Living the Dream, Serving the Queen

Richard M. Jones

ISBN 978-1-716-36618-5

Copyright © 2020 by Richard M. Jones

The moral right of the author has been asserted.

All rights reserved.
No part of this publication may be reproduced, distributed, or transmitted in any form or by any means, including photocopying, recording, or other electronic or mechanical methods, without the prior written permission of the publisher, except in the case of brief quotations embodied in critical reviews. For permission requests, please email the publisher.

A CIP catalogue record for this book is available from the British Library.

Front cover design donated by an artist who wishes to remain anonymous, not for reproduction without permission from the publisher.
Images in this book are the property of the contributors.

Edited and published by Juliette Jones Editorial Services
Juliette.jones@outlook.com
www.juliettejones.co.uk

Dedicated to those who serve in the Royal Navy.

Past, present and future.

Also by Richard M. Jones

The Great Gale of 1871

Lockington - Crash at the Crossing

The Burton Agnes Disaster

End of the Line - The Moorgate Disaster

Capsized in the Solent - The SRN6-012 Hovercraft Disaster

Royal Victoria Rooms - The Rise and Fall of a Bridlington Landmark

The Diary of a Royal Marine – The Life and Times of George Cutcher

Boleyn Gold (fiction)

Collision in the Night – The Sinking of HMS Duchess

RMS Titanic – The Bridlington Connections

Austen Secret (fiction)

Contents

Introduction .... P. 1
    Frederick Harder .... P. 3
    Brian Marlow .... P. 50
    Fred West .... P. 60
    Albert Calland .... P. 64
    Harry and Michael Milne .... P. 68
    Steve Mathis .... P. 79
    Ellen Turner .... P. 91
    Keith Cooper .... P. 94
    Simon Bloomfield .... P. 96
    Martin Barmby .... P. 110
    Robert Lawes .... P. 120
    Richard Jones .... P. 122
    Sam Shannon .... P. 142
Epilogue .... P. 146

Introduction

In December 2019 a deadly virus had started to impact the lives of people the world over. By March 2020 the UK had resorted to a national lockdown.

So, while everybody was forced to stay at home, away from relatives and friends, I had an idea – one that I hoped would particularly benefit the veterans now facing not only physical but social isolation.

As somebody who has written about forgotten aspects of history for over a decade I figured that now was the time to ask the people of Britain to submit their memories of the time they served in the Royal Navy. I reached out on social media for people to get in touch and within hours I had stories from sailors who could now provide a cross section of decades of service from the 1950s onwards from surface fleet, submariners and WRNS.

I joined the navy in 1998 and since then I have seen so many changes to the fleet; the personnel, the way they do things, the deployments, the rules ... the list is endless. It got me thinking a long time ago that if this is what has changed in twenty years imagine what stories are out there from the Second World War onwards.

It is over a decade now since the final veteran of the First World War passed away and as the years tick by the stories of naval history are being lost forever unless something is done about it.

In 2018 my family and I attended Armed Forces Day in Portsmouth and we were pleased to see the nearby D-Day Museum was open. I was very excited to see that three actual veterans of 6th June 1944 were sat in the entrance, ready to share their stories; to my dismay nobody was engaging with them!

This was an opportunity that I wasn't going to miss and we immediately chatted to them, shook their hands and had our photo taken with these heroes of World War II. I am glad I did, one of them, John Jenkins, has died recently at the age of 100.

So, this book is not only a dedicated to those who have served in the past but to those who take the time to talk to veterans and gather the stories up.

History like this should not be left to be forgotten.

Richard M. Jones
August 2020

Left to right: John Jenkins (Gold Beach), Freddie Homard (Sword Beach) and Joe Cattini (Gold Beach).

Fred Harder

As a Boy I always wanted to be either a Farmer or a sailor but living in Southampton it had to be a sailor. At a young age when Mum took us to the seaside (Weston) or Dad took me further afield to Bexhill or other places in his work, I would hold my hands as if they were binoculars and look out to sea and imagine that I was at sea with no land in sight.

After leaving school I had a couple of jobs which only lasted a short time; the first as a plater's boy at Camper and Nicholson's shipyard in Northam that only lasted a few weeks as they wanted me to be an apprentice earning 19s 6d, less than I could get as a paper boy.

From there I had a job over in Totton, the other side of Southampton, at an engineering firm and cycling from Northam, a matter of about 8 miles. The job consisted of standing at a vice all day long filing different aluminium objects to get the casting burr from them. I was asked to leave there as I was taking a lot of time off going around the shipping offices; there were quite a few, from Cunard, Blue Star down to the Red Funnel Steamers.

I then got a job at the top of St Marys road in "James Electric Bakery"; the only things electric were the mixer and the lights. Some of the jobs that I had to perform were to punch out the pastry bases for the tarts and fill them with jam, lemon curd or almond paste, and to fill cream horns with jam and cream. I remember once I had to make a batch of hot cross buns. I made the dough, rolled out the buns, placed them on their tray and put the crosses on them, putting them in the steam proofer to help them raise a bit then into the oven. When I went to take them out they were flat and burnt; I had forgotten to put any sugar into them. One of the men I worked with used to be a head baker on the *Queen Mary*, and another who was a bit like that, escaped to England from a prisoner of war camp in Germany dressed as a woman. During my meal breaks I was still going around the shipping offices as I still wanted to go to sea, so after trying to get into the Merchant Navy with no luck (to this day I am pleased that I didn't) I decided to try for the Royal Navy.

There was a naval recruiting office in Orchard Place opposite the dockyard gate in Southampton; I cycled down there and asked if I could join up. When I told them my age they said I would have to join as a Boy. I was told to attend an interview but I must first have my parents' written consent to join. Dad was not very pleased for me to join the navy as most of my relations were ex-army but Mum talked him into signing the papers, so I duly attended the interview with my signed chitty in my hand.

There was a basic test of arithmetic and reading plus a little basic test on common sense things, like they gave you a picture of a handsaw and underneath was a drawing of a brick, iron, wood, a few other things and asked what you would use the saw to cut. I'm not the brightest of people, but I passed with flying colours and was told to attend again in a couple of weeks' time 'to sign up' and not to bring anything with me except the things I would be wearing.

I rushed home to tell Mum, who of course knew that her big son would pass.

The day came for me to leave home on 7th March 1950 with the normal goodbyes. Mum waved to me going up the street to catch the tram into town. When I arrived at the recruiting office there were about fifteen other boys there; to my surprise one was my cousin from Honeysuckle Road, and another was Sandy Martin, a pal who lived just up the top of the road from me and who attended Sea Cadets at the same time as me. We were all mustered by name then we were all taken by Royal Navy Lorry to the Southampton Central Station where we caught a train to Fareham and changed for Gosport (this was before all the trains were cut and they still went to Gosport). At Gosport we were met by another Royal Navy lorry which took us through the town to H.M.S. St Vincent, a very imposing establishment.

We were driven through a big archway which opened onto an extremely large parade ground surrounded by high walls with at one end tall red buildings in front of which was a very tall mast.

H.M.S. St Vincent Gosport Main Gate

St Vincent Parade ground and mast. (Very old Photo) Officers in dress coats but otherwise nothing has changed.

We were driven across the parade ground to the New Entry annex where we met up with other boys who had come from all over the country to join up. I was now in the Navy as Boy Seaman 2nd Class Frederick Harder, official number JX 882865, but it would still be some time before I went to sea.

We were all fallen in (in a manner of speaking) and then split up into groups to form messes (dorms) and then into classes. I was placed into New Entry Division, Hood class. We were then taken to the clothing store and issued with our uniforms. First we were given a large kit bag, followed by two complete uniforms, one for best and one for working (No Number 8's uniform, we were issued with overalls), then two of each of everything - blue collars, a black silk, lanyards, white fronts, black jersey, vests, underpants, socks, stockings, two hats (one black, one white), plus a metal hat box to keep them in so that they would not get out of shape, two pairs of boots (one pair for working and marching, the 2nd as best), slippers, pumps and football boots, sportswear including shorts and long sleeved jumpers. Then there was a blue kind of bag which was called a 'house wife' which contained everything needed to sew and repair your kit from needle and cotton to buttons, black and white tape and wool (to darn your socks).

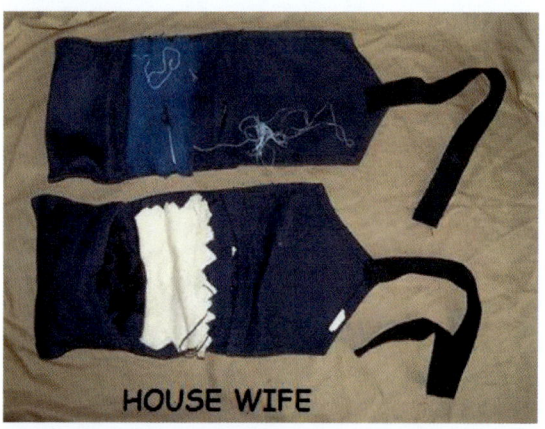
HOUSE WIFE

The list continues with two boot brushes (with black and brown boot polish) and a clothes brush, blue gloves and a black woollen scarf that could be turned into a hat, green military belt and gaiters. We were then issued a money belt then onto a counter where they gave you two towels, a flannel, a bar of soap for washing your clothes and a bar of ordinary soap, tooth brush and paste (a pink powder in a little tin, no tubes in those days), a shaving brush, shaving soap and a cut throat razor (no safety razors), a comb and brush and a small attaché case.

By this time the kit bag was getting quite full (and Heavy) but they had not finished; there was a heavy navy coat of thick wool and an oilskin (for wet weather) then onto bedding. Two thick, rough wool blankets and a couple of pillowcases and a Royal Navy counterpane (no sheets or pyjamas; it would be a few years before they supplied them, you slept under blankets in your underwear), two mattress covers. There was no Hammock or clues (the thin rope strands at the end of the hammock to tie it to the sky hooks) or lashings, you got those when you were getting ready to go to sea.

Finally you were given a seamanship manual, a Bible and a large military respirator (gas mask which went over your head and had a long pipe to a filter which was contained in a canvas shoulder bag).

With all our kit and our kitbag over our shoulders we were ushered into our mess and allocated a bed and locker. We dumped our kit onto our beds and were then made to strip naked and place all our civilian clothes and any possessions that we had with us into a large brown box and make it into a parcel; we had to brown tape it up and put our home address on and send it home. We were all in the noddy and you could tell the kids that were not used to being that way in company. We were then taken to the shower room where we had to shower and then go to the barbers for a haircut.

Back in the mess we were shown how to dress in our nice new uniforms. I and a couple of other lads who had been in the Sea Cadets knew how to dress so when we were fully dressed helped those that were getting in a muddle, as it can be quite a job getting all your uniform on in the correct way.

We were then taken to the mess hall and given a meal and afterwards we were given a lecture by the OIC (Officer in Charge) telling us that we were in the greatest service and that we had to work hard to become sailors of the King. When that was finished we returned to our mess and were shown how to make up our beds in the naval style which was to fold them into themselves making it look neat at both ends with four layers. We were then told to get undressed and to turn in for a well-earned sleep. During the night you could hear a few of the younger kids crying as it was their first time away from their mothers and home so they were home sick.

The next morning we were woken by the blast of a bugle call and our instructor Petty Officer shouting, "Wakey! Wakey! Rise and shine the morning's fine, out you get!" He then turned over the beds of the boys who were slow in getting out and then proceeded to show us how we should make our beds up in the Naval style.

Everything had to be taken off the bed; the counterpane was then placed over the mattress and tucked in tight, the blankets had to be folded in a particular way so that there were four folds instead of the normal two, then the pillows on top. Many years later when we were issued pyjamas they would be rolled up and placed in front of the blanket and pillows.

When we had mastered the blanket folding, we had our breakfast in the mess hall. We were kept away from the old salts, who had been there over the six week training period, then we were taken to be issued with an identity disc (fire proof so that if the worst came to the worst and we were burnt, you could be identified) to be placed around our neck, never to be removed.

We were then taken into a room with benches and a sailor gave us a strip of wood and some little blocks of wood with the letters of our name in type which was made up into a wooden block with your name in reverse. Back in the mess we were given two pieces of surge on which was impregnated with black or white paint, then with our name type and the paint we had to mark every part of our kit with our name; while our boots, shoes, football boots, brushes and cap box were all stamped with our names on. Our kitbags were marked in a similar way but with bigger letters.

After they had all been marked we had to take our kitbag with our name and official number on to have our I.D. photos taken to be placed into our pay book (this gave all your details such as name, date of birth, height, colour of eyes, blood group etc.)

Wooden Name stamp *Name tally for our hat box*

A nice new haircut and uniform. For my I.D./Pay Book

We were then issued with a number of scans of red "ANCHOR" silks, which we had to use to sew with chain stitch every item of our clothing with our name. Most of it had to be done in our own time when not buffing up our boots, washing, ironing and swatting up. Every item when complete had to be shown to the instructor; if he did not like it and it did not look tidy you had to undo it and re-sew it. I was very glad that I never had any other initials than F. Some kids had lots of initials and long names. Some were lucky if they were a Mc something or other and it was long; all they had to do was the Mc and the first letter of their name. Some with short names finished first and for a little fee would sew "X" number of letters for you.

Here in St Vincent we did our first six weeks basic

Hood Class, some classmates I went to Ganges with and some I met in passing, all over the world.

training, learning to dress, wash clothing, clean our brass buttons, Blanco our gaiters, marching, doing all types of formations on the march with or without rifles, plus learn the 24 hour clock plus the naval watch system, then about seamanship tying knots, box the compass, learn all about the parts of a ship, basic navigation and a hell of a lot more. I was lucky; having been a Sea Cadet I knew how to put my uniform on etc. One day we were all taken to the sickbay to have our jabs. Time flew and before long we were allowed out on a Sunday afternoon to walk around Gosport. One day we were all told to dress in our number one dress suit as we were to have our photos taken.

The "M" over the nose.

With some of my mates.

Standing alongside my cousin.

My cousin, I think, made it through his course but I never met up with him; while Sandy Martin, the friend I signed on with, never lasted the six week course.

We had a lot of sport activities, the first being that we were all lined up by size to form two lines, red and blue. Each pair had to enter the boxing ring and beat the hell out of each other for three minutes. The person judged to have won (me) had his hand lifted above his head and the next pair took over. We had to participate in all the games; hockey, rugby, football, cross country running etc.

Also we had to take swimming lessons and at the end had to do a test to get our swimming proficiency certificate. This entailed being dressed in a white duck suit made of light canvas and having to swim a couple of lengths of the bath then duck dive to the bottom in the deep end and recover a heavy object and then swim on your back with this weight on your chest to the side and give it to the instructor. I, and a few others that could swim, passed the test the first time round and had our pay book noted to the effect that we had successfully passed the test, but there were quite a few non swimmers who had to take extra lessons in the evenings or early mornings.

On one weekend the New Entry Division was opened up to visitors and our parents were invited to visit the establishment. My Mum and Dad came down and watched us doing our parade marching and then they had a look around our accommodation and classrooms, then had tea with sticky buns before being driven to the station. I think that they were very proud of how I was getting on.

H.M.S. Victory Portsmouth dockyard

As our basic training as Boy Seamen 2nd class progressed, we were taken on a visit to *H.M.S. Victory*. It was every boy's dream as we marched through the dockyard, arms swinging to our shoulders, being watched by all the salted sailors from all the different ships decks.

There were a great many warships tied up alongside the jetties; there were cruisers, destroyers, frigates submarines and minesweepers, while the biggest one was the battleship *H.M.S. King George V*, which to us was massive.

H.M.S. King George V

As our training course in H.M.S. St Vincent was coming to an end and our exams and tests had been passed, not everyone made it, we were told that as boys we could either become Seamen and at a later date choose the branch/profession that we wished to go into, or become Boy Communicators and after a basic training in HMS Ganges could become communicators, specialising as a Radio Operator or Visual as a Signalman. A number of us volunteered and were chosen to do a Morse aptitude test to become a communicator. I was one of the chosen ones.

First our hearing and sight were again tested and had to be 100%, then we went into a classroom for the test. The test comprised of having sounds played to us over a radio and being told that one dit (.) was the letter 'E' while one dash (-) was the letter 'T' and a few other basic combinations of dits and dashes. These symbols were played to us a number of times and then we had to write down the letters which was then marked by the instructor. I must have been in the top number as I was selected with a few others to be trained as a Communicator either as Signalman (visual, flags, lights, etc) called 'Buntings' (as flags were made of bunting) or Radio Telegraphists reading Morse and anything to do with radio communications. In the Navy we were called 'Sparkers' as in the early days of radio the valves in the radios sparked to make the required dits and dashes.

Having completed our six weeks basic training, those selected were transported by lorry to Gosport railway station, followed by another lorry with our kit bags to catch the train to London. At London Waterloo we were met by military police with another lorry to take us across London to catch another train for Ipswich, where we were met by a Naval Bus who transported us to H.M.S. Ganges.

H.M.S. Ganges Shotley Main Gate

Ganges figure head and Mast

     We were met on the parade ground by our new instructors and Divisional Officer who gave us a little lecture. On completion we were marched away. I was assigned to and joined Grenville Division (all the divisions were named after famous Admirals) which was situated in a very long covered way with messes on either side.

H.M.S. Ganges - Long covered way (Good for sliding in our hob nail boots)

Shotley & H.M.S. Ganges

I was allocated class 222. The Messes consisted of a single floored building which you entered from the long covered way. On entry there were two little rooms; one was the wash room, the other the 'dhobey' room where you did your clothes washing. Along the passage it opened up to a long dormitory. The first patch was a large square of wooden tiled flooring, white from being scrubbed so many times; this area was the dining area and contained four tables with benches plus a locker to stow your cups etc. There were also the utensils e.g. very large teapot, 'Fannies' for soup, stews porridge etc, "all highly polished, by us of course". You used to go to the galley to collect your victuals and then there was the highly polished wooden floor area with beds either side with a locker alongside each bed where you kept all your clothing clean neat tidy and tied up in rolls.

    We were issued our bedding and given a bed and locker to stow our gear away. We emptied our kit bags; the kit bags went under the mattress with our best bellbottom trousers folded in the regulation manner with seven creases across while turned inside out on top of the kitbag to keep the creases in. Some people smeared pussers (naval issue) soap on the creases to keep them in, it worked, but the soap rotted the material.

    By the time all this was accomplished, it was time for our evening meal. A couple of the lads were detailed off to be the cooks of the mess and go to the galley and collect the evening meal. The tea was made in a big 'Fanny' by placing a couple of hands full of tea, sugar and carnation milk and taking it to the galley for hot water. We were all issued with a plate, mug and knife and fork. We had to mark the plate and mug with our initials; this was done by pouring a drop of vinegar on the item and then with a piece of aluminium scrape out the initials, it works. After our meal we had to wash up and stow all the gear.

On our arrival we had been introduced to our instructors. I think mine was Acting Petty Officer Hammond, who was still in the same uniform as us, who fell us into a squad and we had to march around the establishment having points of interest shown to us to remember. On completion of the tour, we were marched back to our messes and made to turn in.

There was more basic training: e.g. learn to read the Morse code and progress in speed, at the same time learning how to type. We started with the middle line on the typewriter with the letters 'a' 's' then 's' 'a's on our left hand fingers and thumb then added the symbols and letter with our right hand ';' 'l' then 'l' ';'s on the middle line on the keyboard and progressed to all the keys on the keypad. We were to be touch typists, so we progressed to having all the keys covered with little black caps so you did not know which keys were which.

We then progressed further and had to read the Morse code while typing the letters and figures. At the same time we went to school progressing our Maths, English etc., also we carried on with our seamanship and rope work knots, splices and whipping, navigation, rule of the road, reading the 24 hour clock.

After a time we sat further tests to see who would become Signalmen (flags, flashing light, semaphore and ships manoeuvres) or Telegraphists (Morse code, ciphers, codes and radio equipment). I was selected to be in the telegraph's stream and made up to Boy Telegraphist 2nd Class.

My training in Ganges took 15 months, having been back classed for a few weeks into 233 class. I never could get right the S's 3(dits) ... and H's 4(dits) ....

especially when the speed was upped. But I was O.K. on the 5's which was 5(dits) ..... though.

After a time we had to sit an examination and on passing were issued our branch badges; cross flags for Signalmen (Buntings or Bunce) and flying lightning with wings for the Telegraphists (Sparkers), which we had to sew onto our uniforms. There were also gold badges for our best uniform (No 1's) and red ones for our No 2's and blue and white ones for our working uniform.

Every week a different class had to do guard duty, that is to be ahead of the parade ground and march off etc.

233 Class touch typing and reading Morse on Old imperial typewriters

Grenville Division 1950/1

While in Ganges, I played water polo for the division

I was in the Field Gun's crew and we won medals for the two highest honours, the overall winners and the fastest time.

I was also in the Kings Birthday review guard.

Wednesday afternoon was our half day off. It is called a 'Make and Mend' day (to repair or make things to your kit). But most of all we had to take part in sports. I had to play football, hockey and rugby, take part in cross country running and a few other games.

The G.I. (Gunnery Instructor) wanted me to take up boxing; the reason being that he thought I had it in me to be a boxer was due to an incident one day in the mess. I sat down at the table with a cup of tea and a biscuit or something and this bloke across from me who fancied himself as a boxer (broken nose etc) took the cup and said, "This is mine." I grabbed it back and said, "Oh no it isn't, it's mine." He pulled it towards himself, both of us having hold of the cup at the time and said, "Mine!" This happened a few times backwards and forwards. Then when he did it again I let it go and the hot tea went all over him. He got up and threw a punch, I retaliated, then he put his head down and started flaying his arms all over the place. I put my hand over his head to keep him at bay, and when he lifted his head I hit him once and he fell backwards over the bench. Looking up, there was the G.I. watching us. We were both put in the RATTLE (placed on a charge for fighting) and brought before the Officer of the day on the quarterdeck. We were both given punishment; about three or four days No 7's (I think) having to get up early do cleaning, report every so often, then in the evening after evening instructions run (double) around the parade ground with our rifle's over our heads. We were never alone, there was always quite a few doing 'Jankers' (punishment).

Anyway I could not box as I had what they thought was a weak stomach; one punch and I was knackered. I did as every new recruit had to do in St Vincent, that is to 'box in the mill', as part of your training. One class is given blue ribbons to tie around their waist the other class is given red. Everyone has to go in the ring in turn and box like hell (Blood and snot) against your opponent for three minutes, the ref then says which one had won, it was then the turn of the next two to enter the ring. (I did win my bout).

Life in Ganges was quite hectic, reveille bugle call would go about 06.30 followed by the same music every day; one was "If you roll a silver dollar down upon the ground it will roll roll roll," must have been the current number one. It was then a mad rush to wash, normally in cold water. If you were boat party, you had to get up earlier and go sailing or rowing on the river, come rain, snow or shine.

Some of the older boys shaved, so we were all issued with shaving gear and cut-throat razors; I gave mine to my Dad. You had to make up your bedding - all the blankets and sheets all folded in regimental style with your name showing. If you were duty cook you had to go up to the galley and collect a fanny of tea, the breakfast and bread and butter, then dish it out in the mess, then afterwards wash and clean the dishes and place them on display in the open shelves.

You Normally would then Muster outside your mess and report to the duty Officer that everything was correct, no boys had gone missing etc and then you would be double marched away to instruction. Sometimes everyone would fall in on the parade ground for prayers etc.

Every few weeks you would have to muster your kit and lay it out on the deck in a regimental style, as laid out in the seamanship manual.

Once a week we would have to do our washing in the wash house. We would all have to strip and were allocated a large sink and soap to do our washing. Most times the water would be cold and they would swish the water all over the place. First the whites, white fronts, vests, hankies and underpants; the underpants were the worst to wash (scrub) as they were the long ones that came to your knees, no Y fronts in those days. Also, because all our blue surge uniforms were new, when you sweated (which was often after doubling all around the camp) the dye would transfer to your underpants and under your armpits on the white fronts; you would scrub them until you thought they were clean, then take them to the instructor who would inspect and if they were not clean enough he would dip them in the cold water and hit you with them, so you had to go back and rewash before putting them in the dryer.

The following photo must have been taken some time ago as we never had canvas trousers (only for our swimming test).

This is an old photo; I expect they have their pants on because of the photo.

      Every so often, we would have to take tests, or exams in reading Morse, by pencil and on typewriter, touch typing, sending morse on a key, reading and sending flashing lights, know the colours of all flags and their Naval and international meaning, the basic formations of ships, read semaphore, how to use codes and code books. At the same time there was our educational test in Maths, English, Magnetism and Electrics, plus our marching and arms drills and of course our kit musters. At the end of one of the tests I was made up from Boy Telegraphist to Ordinary Telegraphist, giving me a little more pay.

      Later on in our becoming sailors, we spent a day on a warship just to see what it was like and get the feel of being at sea. The ship that my class were taken to was *H.M.S. Bleasdale*, a fine looking Destroyer. I will always remember, we all had to take a bag meal with us (most had eaten what they had in their bags before we even got on board) and at dinnertime we were sat round a mess table (a trellis of planks of wood scrubbed until they were nearly white) on a metal frame which could be broken down and stowed away in emergencies, when one of the sailors brought us a tray of "Manchester tart" pastry with lashings of red jam covered in a thick custard with coconut chips on top... lovely.

H.M.S. Bleasdale, the first ship I ever went on.

Three times a year we would be given two weeks leave. On leave mornings we would be up very early, about 4ish, the duty cook would go to the galley and collect a fanny of KIE which was a very thick Coco, and a packet of hard (*very* hard) ships biscuits for each of us. Then we would have to strip and have a shower in the very cold shower room with even colder water. As you can guess we tried not to stay there too long, but the instructors watched us so we had to show willing. It was then back to the mess to change into our best uniforms, then fall in (muster) on the parade ground to have our pay, our victualing allowance (to give to Mum for our keep for the two weeks) our ration coupons, as some things were still rationed, and our train warrant. When that was completed we all had to muster by destinations, e.g. Waterloo for those going to London and the South. We then got onto buses which took us to Ipswich station, there a mad rush to get to the platform and onto the train, you can just imagine hundreds of kid sailors running around shouting laughing and making a noise. I bet they were very glad that it was only three times a year.

Mum was always pleased to see me in my nice uniform, her first job was to get all my clothing and boil them in her boiler until they were shiny, starched white and clean.

Coming to the end of our course after all our examinations etc had been passed. At the end of our course we were all allocated our drafts; if you were going to the Home Fleet you just wore your normal uniform, but if you were going abroad you were issued with your white uniforms (again marking all your kit and sewing your name in). Most of the class were drafted to *H.M.S. Forth* in Malta which was a submarine base ship. Bill Bailey and myself were drafted to the Mediterranean Fleet to *H.M.S. Mermaid*, the leader of the 2nd Frigate squadron based in Malta.

We sailed from Liverpool on the troopship *Empress of Australia* and had quite a good time as the Sgt Major did not know what to do with us sailors. We visited our first foreign port, which was Gibraltar, never having been into bars with saw dust on the floors and all the noise and women around. It was great; we looked round the shops and bought sweets and chocolate, which was still rationed back home, visited a few bars and had a couple of beers while taking in the atmosphere. It was then back on board for the long haul through the

Mediterranean to Malta. You could see it in the distance, all it was is a great chunk of brownish rock.

When we disembarked in Grand Harbour in Malta the *Mermaid* was still at sea, so we were taken to H.M.S. Ricasoli to await her return. H.M.S. Ricasoli is/was a large fort at the entrance to Grand Harbour; here we were billeted in the old stables which were built of large sandstone blocks, the ceilings were very high which was great as it kept the place cool. The walls of the parade ground reflected the sun so if you stood on parade for a time it was very exhausting.

HMS Amethyst of the Yangtze river incident (like Mermaid) in Grand Harbour, with HMS Ricasoli (back left) old fort.

While we waited for the ship to come in we had to do Morse exercises and general cleaning duties. One thing that I can remember was that at tea time and meals we had butter which was still rationed at home. The butter was cut up into small squares and placed into dishes with iced water to keep it firm as it was very hot out there. Sweets and chocolate were also still rationed in England but here in Malta you could go into any shop or vendor's tent and get what you wanted; so I made a parcel of sweets to send home to Mum, but before I could fill the parcel (constrained by cash) it came over the BBC that sweet ration had been abolished, so I ate what I had bought, and must have put on a few pounds.

We were kept busy while we waited for the *Mermaid*, we would spend some time in cleaning ship then we would spend more time in the classroom doing Morse and typing tests. In the evening we would either go out for a drink or walk along the battlement.

Mermaid in Grand Harbour Malta. 1952

Finally the day came and we watched *Mermaid*, our ship, sail past the entrance to Grand harbour and enter Sliema creek, which was her normal anchorage, tied up between two buoys alongside (some of the time) to a couple of other Frigates or Destroyers. That is when we had a navy.

Sliema creek at the top of the picture.

We were taken by lorry through Valletta and around the coastline to the waterfront at Sliema where there were lots of Frigates and Destroyers tied up to Buoys in the middle of the creek with ship's boats plying between ships and shore. There were lots of local boats called Dghajsa (Die-sa), which are boat taxis. Most ships had their own local Dghajsa which would take people ashore or bring them from the shore to the ship, thereby saving calling the ship's motorboat away.

We were picked up by the ships boat and taken to the *Mermaid*. We had all our kit with us, kitbag, hammock and little case. As we went over the gangway and saluted the quarterdeck, as we had been taught to do at Ganges, the noise and bustle was overbearing. The noise of the engines and all the fans and extractor fans giving off an eternal hum, the crew were storing ship, a lighter (barge) was alongside and as the stores were hoisted aboard there were a long line of sailors, including Petty Officers etc, who passed the packages from one to the other to disappear down below to be stowed. The packages were made up with all manner of things from potatoes to eggs, bread, milk, plus the NAAFI stores of sweeties, cigs, canned drinks etc. while at the same time taking on water and fuel from lighters alongside.

We dodged the workers along the upper deck and were shown to our messes. Clanking down steep, steel ladders into the bowels of the ship, Bill and I were now separated. He was going to the Boys' mess and me as an Ordinary Telegraphist was shown to the Communications and Misc (cooks, stores ratings etc) mess deck.

It seemed very strange at first; it was an open deck, a wide open space from one side to the other side of the ship split into messes. My mess was on the port side of the ship, comprising two wooden trestle tables with metal legs which were secured into mounts on the deck by brass pins so that they did not slide along when the ship was in bad weather. They could be disassembled very quickly and secured on the deck head in a matter of seconds when going to action stations so that the decks would be clear.

On one side of the tables there was a wooden bench (you learn to sleep on these when off watch) and on the other side all along the deck were cushions on top of a kind of long bench which were split into boxes which were our lockers; so if someone was asleep on top of your locker and you wished to get something out they were not very pleased if you had to shake them. There was a metal cupboard on the bulkhead with a number of shelves on top with metal guards across to support the crockery and cooking utensils as the ship was 'Canteen messing' or 'Broadside' messing, meaning that the food was brought from the canteen and you had to prepare it yourselves and take it to the galley to be cooked.

A More modern Mess, which has cushions on the benches.

Our plate stowage had no doors. The lockers are under the seats and all the plates etc were white.

Under the ladder leading to the next deck up were the Hammock Nettings, which consisted of a metal cage where you stowed your hammocks like a load of cigars when not in use during the day. In the centre of the open deck was a large square cabin-like structure which was the sick bay where the Sick Berth Attendant looked after the sick and needy.

I was introduced to the killick (Leading Hand) of the mess who allocated me a locker and sky hooks to sling my hammock, there were not many ratings in the mess at this time as most of them were storing ship, but the couple who were there introduced themselves. I was told to stow my hammock in the hammock net (remembering that I had had to carry my bedding with me a quarter way around the world along with my kitbag and small attaché case) and leave my kitbag to be unpacked later.

I was then taken up ladders and along gangways to the B.W.O. (Bridge Wireless Office) which was alongside the Captain's cabin. It was a pokey little place; along one side was a bench with typewriters in little groves, alongside was a space for writing messages alongside a Morse key. Above the bench was a shelf with B28 and B29 radio receivers, while at the other end of the office was a big blue FM12 D/F Direction Finding set (this I found out was always tuned to 500 kc/s, the distress frequency). Above this was a big brass clock marked out with the silent periods on so that you could listen out for any distress signals.

In the middle of the office was a big black American transmitter, the TBL. On the outer bulkhead was a scuttle with a wind scoop (to scoop cool air when underway). Under this was a big metal cage with a VHF transmitter, with valves the size of two or three footballs; these gave off so much heat that we used them to dry our dhobying. There were a couple of other transmitters, I think 89q which was for emergencies if power was lost. On a bench was the crypto machine, a Type X for decoding message received on the broadcast... plus a few cupboards etc. Outside the door was a metal type of box which held a bank of large batteries which was used for emergency power.

The BWO, not a good photo only a box camera

I was introduced to the P.O. Tel who was to be my boss his name was PO Tel (POTS) Deadman and because the *Mermaid* was a Frigate leader we had a CPO Tel Crossman as well. Also I was introduced to a couple of the sparkers who were on watch. One of them was detailed off to show me around the ship.

The first place that he took me to, which was the most important, was the canteen. Important because if you did not like the meals that the "Cook of the Mess dished up" you would go to the canteen for something to eat, like a can of cold beans or "'errings in tomato sauce". There were things like D.F's duty free cigarettes, nutty, soups etc. The canteen flat also held a "Goffer" machine, which served up cold drinks, and a drinking water fountain.

NAAFI canteen

From here I was taken to the bathroom which I was to use, this consisted of a number of stainless steel hand basins down one side and on the other a number of shower cubicles. I found out later that the showers could be fresh water in harbour and mostly at sea, but if fresh water become rationed then the showers would be made to use salt water. You were given salt water soap (never did get much of a froth with it) to use. On the deck were duck boards, wooden hatch covers that you could stand on; when in a drop of rougher's the water would slop out of the basins and wash over the deck from side to side.

Here in the morning you would rush to have a shave etc, do your washing mostly in a bucket, scrub your hammock or kitbag on the deck. In good weather you would sit on a bollard on deck and do your dhobying (washing). When you had done your dhobying, you would take it to the fo'c'sle where there would be lines of rope stretched across where you would tie your washing with seaming twine (clothes pegs were no good); if you were at sea and did not do a very good job of it then your articles would fly away and the Captain would not turn round to retrieve them. When at sea some of the crew would tie their hammocks to a heaving line and string them over the stern to wash them, if you left it there the correct amount of time, it would come out a lovely clean colour, but if you forgot it overnight all that would be left would be the brass eye, the rest would have been worn away.

Our next port of call was the heads (WC). We stepped over the hatching and along one side were a set of urinals with again duckboards on the deck, while on the other side was a bank of box type compartments risen off the deck by about 18" on a shelf like structure. The compartments were about 3 ft high with two little doors with an over catch to them containing a toilet. They were risen off the deck so that in bad weather water would not slop around your ankles and wet your trousers. When sitting on the toilet your chest and shoulders would be above the compartment so that you could talk to your oppo; I think the reason for this was so that people could not skive. Anyone looking through the door would see who was on the loo. At this time there were no nice soft toilet paper! There was a little wooden box with what appeared to be 6" squares of brown wrapping paper, which they called "Admiralty Browns" or "Pussers wipes". These squares, like wrapping paper, were rough on one side and smooth on the other. I think at one time each sheet was stamped with an Admiralty fouled anchor.

In our two and a half years commission we visited most of the countries having a shoreline. In those days the Fleet sailed out of Malta on cruises, consisting the Spring, Summer and Winter cruises. The places visited was normally with your own squadron, but at some point, the Fleet met up and we had a regatta, where each department rowed or sailed against the same department on other ships. I was in one of the communications team who came in 2nd or 3rd and we had to go aboard the flagship and receive our prize of about 4 shilling each from the Countess Mountbatten. We also carried out evolutions which in some cases were very funny, but in others quite serious, especially in the communications world as Louis Mountbatten kept us on our toes.

In our time on the *Mermaid*, both Bill and I had temporary draft of one kind or another. I think Bill went on *H.M.S. Magpie*, while I went on the aircraft carrier *H.M.S. Ocean* who had a crash sailing to the Eastern Med where there was trouble with (I think it was still called) Palestine and Egypt. We called into Cyprus where we had to wait for some reason, and while I and a few others on a bicycle trip were in a bar up the mountain, over the radio they broadcasted the death of the King.

We never did get any further; the *Ocean* was recalled and I rejoined my ship. Another temp draft I had was to take passage from Gibraltar, where we were doing a refit, to Malta on the American Submarine *USS Requin*. The reason being that there had been a massive earthquake in Greece and H.M.S. Camorata, the communications centre in Malta, required more operators to man the additional nets.

When that was over and the *Mermaid* returned to Malta. I rejoined her and a short time after we sailed to do convoy duties in the Suez Canal which entailed escorting convoys from Port Said to Port Tawfik while another convoy came from the other way, meeting and passing in the Bitter lakes. This we carried out many, many times, most of the time we were at actions stations. After our stint in Egypt, we visited many places, passed through the Corinth Canal, visited Venice and went up into the

Dolomite mountains, Italy, Sicily, Cannes, Monte Carlo and many other places.

Not long after we sailed to England with the squadron to attend the Spithead review. While we were there in our positions we were passed by the "*John Biscoe*", the Antarctic research vessel. On board was my brother Desmond, who was a cabin boy on there.

After the review we returned to the Med and did a few exercises with the Americans. At one stage an American Dakota with 32 people on board ditched and *Magpie* and *Mermaid* were rushed to pick them up; meanwhile a sea plane had landed alongside and taken the 32 people off prior to the Dakota sinking. The seaplane can only carry 12 men, so there were 40 people all hanging onto the plane. Two destroyers, *HMS Saintes* and *Cheviot*, arrived before us and took off most of the women and children. We took the remaining people off and they were showered and fed etc. By this time the sea was getting a bit rough, the only people left on the seaplane were the crew. Most of them being sea sick, one was even coughing up blood, the plane could not take off due to the weather. A whaler was launched but could not get close to the plane so the crew broke out the rubber dinghy's. The liner *Asturias* then came along to help and took all the passengers aboard and proceeded to Malta.

We abandoned the plane to its own fate and headed for Tobruk but received a message telling us to go back and tow the plane. Anyway, after a lot of bother, ropes snagging and breaking in the rough seas, in the end we turned over the tow to *HMS Loch Lomond* but the final outcome was that the plane sank due to the weather.

On our return to Malta I was sent to Ricasoli to do my Telegraphist's course and was rated up. On my return to the U.K. after leave I was drafted to Mercury for three months before joining *HMS Fleetwood,* part of the

Portsmouth Squadron and experimental ship for ASWE etc. We had to do trials on weapons, and anything new to the Navy. At one time we had to do trials on stabilisers so we had to find bad weather to carry out the trials. The first encounter we had the stabilisers were engaged, but we rocked and rolled worse than without them. It was found that they had been connected wrong and worked in reverse.

We also carried out the first trials with the BID's (equipment for broadcast encryption). I was only on the *Fleetwood* for six months then sent to Mercury for my Leading Tels course. I was then drafted to *HMS Loch Fada* of the Persian Gulf Squadron. We did our work up at Portland with all the evolutions etc. By this time I had started to do a bit of photography, only contact printing at this stage.

*

Fred was Radio Supervisor (known as POTS) on board *HMS Puma* for this next incident -

I was on *HMS Puma* anchored off Jamaica in 1969 after a good run ashore in my whites; the waves and troughs of the Atlantic were very high. You had to jump for your life to reach the gangway which was not very easy with only the gangway lights. Anyway, I came off shore expecting to turn in as it was quite late, but the Quarter Master said, "Hey POTS the skipper wants to see you."

I went up to his cabin, him in pyjamas, he said "POTS there is a merchant ship out there whose Radio Operator has gone sick and needs you to communicate with the U.K. I am sending you and the Doc over there to look after their Radio Operator."

"Yes sir!" says I, and away I go. It was quite difficult even to get into the ship's boat due to the high swell and winds. We got a little wet and the trip was rough and bloody awful; even worse getting onto the merchant ship. In a trough you could nearly see the keel and in the waves you were nearly on their deck, we both jumped for our lives on the topping of a wave but we managed it, we were met by the skipper.

I was taken to the Radio Office while the Doc was taken to the sick bay. I had never seen the Merchant Navy radio equipment but managed to switch on and tune it into Portishead calling frequency (bit easier than Pussers equipment).

I established communications with Portishead and passed the required messages to the company's H.Q. to let them know of the plight of their operator. It turned out that the Radio Operator was a woman and she had had a miscarriage. The Doc sorted her out, the skipper said thank you for all your effort and gave the Doc a bottle of Scotch, and said to me - "I know you are not allowed to have spirit aboard so here is a carton of cigarettes." The trip back was even worse than getting there, we were both wet and very tired by the time we turned in. With the coming of dawn, the next day I got a "Well done POTS," from the skipper.

Brian Marlow

Brian Marlow was only a boy when he joined the Royal Navy in the September of 1956 aged just 15 years old. He would be classed as a junior until he reached the age of 18 and only then would he take on a full rank, but this would not stop him from signing up as a junior Marine Engineer at the gates of HMS Ganges for the start of his boys service.

His journey to these gates had begun a long time ago, his parents had divorced when he was very young and he ended up going to Bournemouth where he joined the Sea Cadets. They would tell him all kinds of stories about how the Navy would take you to all the far reaches of the world while getting paid to do it.

Brian Marlow, HMS Ganges 1957

During his school days he tended to play truant a lot, there was nothing he wanted in the classrooms. All his friends were about to start an apprenticeship for the next five years in a factory, he would be going the same way and he decided that there was no way he was going down that road.

So, one day he bunked off school and headed down to the recruiting office and decided there and then that he would join up. He was accepted and soon found himself stood proud after completing his first part of his year-long training.

After Ganges he would head off to HMS Raleigh in Torpoint for some engineering training before once again being sent to another base, this time the barracks at HMS Victory (today it is HMS Nelson) in Portsmouth.

Brian Marlow & Rod Taylor, HMS Ganges 1957

After a year of training and being held on shore he was finally given a temporary draft, the Second World War battleship *HMS Vanguard*, which was laid up in Portsmouth harbour in reserve status. On here he was marvelling at the size of the vessel… she was huge! Although he was just here to do random jobs and things that required using spare manpower, he loved being on board. "It was marvellous!" he would say in 2020.

HMS Vanguard (photo US Navy)

Brian Marlow, HMS Ceylon

  He would only spend a month or two on here before he was given his first real draft, to the cruiser *HMS Ceylon*, in 1958. At the time he joined she was in dry dock being fitted out ready for her to be recommissioned into the fleet again.

  Ceylon was a lot different to the *Vanguard,* but he soon got working in his core role as a marine engineer. He found that the stokers on there did a bit of everything – working in the boiler room, refrigeration equipment, engine room and the diesel generators, which were always working even when alongside to provide the ship with power.

  Before too long the ship was ready to head back to sea and this is the point where he realised that his decision to head out alone and join the Navy had been the best one. The *Ceylon* put to sea and he found himself going to places that he had never dreamt of heading to. They took the last British troops out of Jordan and ferried them all down to Mombasa. King Hussein came on board for a visit and as Far East Flagship there was always a high ranking admiral coming and going.

HMS Ceylon

As part of relationship building around the globe, the Royal Navy have always made goodwill visits and took part in multi-national exercises with foreign ships and this trip was no different. Brian loved every minute of it and even though it was hard work, he described it today as having "a whale of a time."

On this trip he decided to start getting tattoos as mementoes of his time away, in Hong Kong he got quite a lot more. His 20th birthday was celebrated on board with a tot of rum and he knew he was doing things and seeing places that his schoolfriends would never ever have the chance to see.

Near the Suez Canal two ships had collided and the *Ceylon* was tasked to take a load of metal plates to the scene in order for the crew to effect repairs. By the time they had got there one had already been towed away but the repairs were started on the other and the ship was saved. Around five years after this Brian would get a cheque for 12 shillings and 6 pence salvage money.

It would be 18 months before the ship returned to Portsmouth, which was a standard time away back then. There would be no flights home halfway through the deployment, instead you would simply get about your job and work hard for your next promotion. It was now December when the ship came alongside Portsmouth and he would leave the *Ceylon* with happy memories to take his leave and to head off to his next draft.

Brian Marlow, HMS Ceylon 1959

This time he was going west to serve at HMS Osprey, a shore base in Portland which would be a training establishment for anti-submarine warfare. He would only be there for a short while, accommodated at the barracks on Portland Bill. Nearby was his next draft in the harbour – the more modern ASW frigate *HMS Keppel* which was based right here.

Aboard the 310 foot long *Keppel*, the ship's company would sail the vessel in and around the Lyme Bay area with the submarines to exercise. The frigate would try and detect the sub while the sub would try and evade the frigate in order to get in to simulate an attack. It was good training and a lot of work was done to make sure these exercises would gain maximum training benefit.

Another job they would do was the fishery protection off the coast of Iceland as well as more multi-nation exercises involving ships that would head over to the UK waters for the opportunity to simulate war scenarios. In one such exercise in the North Sea Brian remembers that the captain was a member of the Fleet Air Arm. A storm warning had come in and the ship went to anchor to ride out the bad weather. Unfortunately, the following day the anchor could not be raised for some reason and they had to break the cable and lose the anchor. For the next two days the sea was rough and the ship took a lot of damage from the storm. "The Skipper got thrown over the coals for that!" he remembered.

But then came a part of the ships life that was a little different.

"I was on *Keppel* while they were making a film with Charlie Drake on. None of the cast liked him, he stayed in a big hotel on the sea front with a Rolls Royce there to pick him up and he sometimes never showed up. Victor Maddern one of the actors – got him down the mess at Tot Time and got him pissed – we got in trouble for that. The film company reported that he was drunk, he told him, "I've been down with the sailors" and they were not impressed. Petticoat Pirates it was called. We got new sets of No 8's because the actors would swap their new 8's with the sailors older worn ones."

Before too long he had proved his worth as an able rating and was promoted to Leading Hand. He was sent on draft back to Portsmouth where he did his killicks course over in Gosport at the marine engineering training base HMS Sultan. After successfully completing that he was once again given a ship – this time the aircraft carrier *HMS Hermes* which was yet another ship he would join while in dry dock.

The year was 1962 and as he stepped on board the huge ship for the first time his first impression was that "it was a hell of a mess, dockies everywhere, stuff all

HMS Hermes (Hugh Llewelyn)

over" but he quickly made this ship his home and once again took a ship out of refit and took part in the recommissioning back into the fleet.

The ship then sailed for a long deployment once again where he got down to business keeping watches on the generators.

As the years ticked by, he had got some incredible memories of the places he would go to. When asked what his best run ashore was, he said "Yokohama (Japan)... we had been on a big exercise with different navies and we were going into Tokyo, however because we had admiral on board we went into Yokohama. The Japanese people were brilliant they couldn't do enough for us. They laid on trips to places like Mount Fuji, a beautiful restaurant like a swiss chalet where they laid on a meal. Nothing was too much trouble."

After finishing work, he had the chance to head ashore, but back in those days you didn't wear your civilian clothing unless you were in Portsmouth. "We used to come off watch, put on our uniform, go for a massage/shower ashore, sit at the bar, they'd give you beer, they would give you your clothes back all washed and ironed while you had their dressing gown on."

Brian Marlow , HMS Hermes Stokers Mess 1963

Another run ashore he remembers was Ceylon (now Sri Lanka) where he met a young lady whose father was an Irishman in the local police force and he could get him a job on air conditioning units. However, the evening before the ship sailed, the navy patrol dragged him back to his ship as his mates heard his plan and were worried that he was going to abscond.

Before he had joined the *Hermes* he had got married and by the time he had left the carrier to go on Petty Officer's course he was living nearby in a married quarter close to his base port. She had known he was in the Navy, so they had taken it for what it was and didn't find his job a hassle. But he had signed up for a 12 year career with an opportunity to extend, although as the years had gone by, they discussed the prospects of staying vs leaving. At that point, his wife had said that it was a choice of the Navy or her, so he left around 1967.

Does he regret leaving the Navy? Yes he does. He is no longer married to the woman who was his wife at the time and he says today that his biggest regret is not staying in when he could. He kept in touch with a few old shipmates, one from Ganges only died in 2019, another is now in Australia. He was awarded no medals during his career but is he bitter about his career today? Never! When I asked him what the highlight of his career was he surprised me with a very simple answer.

"Everything! I thoroughly enjoyed it. Life was hard at times but looking back it was worth it." It was here he span a few good stories of his best memories. Like the time when the ship went into Majorca and he went to go back on board with a German sailors' hat on, a huge French roll under his arm and a large bottle of French champagne. He was missing his own cap because he had swapped it. A bit worse for wear, he was locked up in cells for the night, but when he woke up his sentry was in the cell next to him – he had been caught asleep on duty while he was in charge of watching him!

Brian Marlow & Bert Hogarth, Malta 1963

    Another trip had him in the Kenyan city of Mombasa where they could get a bit of leave in the port if the ship was going to be in there for a while. He and about a dozen other shipmates went up country to a bay with a load of camping gear and set up their tents away from anyone that could disturb them. The local natives would leave a pile of fresh fish for them outside the tent for them to enjoy.

    Singapore had him going up to a Gurkha rest camp. Two RAF sergeants used to train people in survival in the jungle and he had agreed to be taken out for the experience. He remembers having to stop every so often and pick leeches off each other before making their camp beds out of branches and wood, or whatever they could scavenge. None of them would sleep though, the noises of splashing in the night could be heard but they couldn't figure out what it was until the next day when the RAF sergeant said, "Did you all see the elephants in the river last night?" Their tents were only a few yards away from the river's edge this entire time!

Fred West
My 24 years in a Blue suit

From an early age I had wanted to join the Navy. My uncle joined the Navy in 1909 as a stoker; he obviously served through the First World War and then decided to sign on for the time between wars. He left the Navy just before the Second World War but volunteered/was asked to come back at the onset of WWII.

He was my inspiration to join, along with a mate I had in the 50's whose dad was again a stoker on submarines. So, the seed was sown and on 30th August 1960 I joined the Navy.

I grew up in Surrey and at the age of 15 my Gran died and my mum was duty bound to go and look after Grandad, who was living in Worthing. So, within a couple of weeks we lifted and shifted to Worthing. I wasn't impressed; I was just about to start my GCE O level year. Anyway we moved and I started school all over again in the 5th year of a school that were miles behind me education wise and for four months I sat there and listened to stuff I had done an age before. I got bored so I took myself to the RN recruiting office in Brighton and took the entrance exam for the RN. I passed and I signed up to join the Royal Navy Electrical Branch.

I went back to school and told my form teacher I had passed the entrance exam for the RN she promptly advised me to leave school as I was wasting my time in school. I didn't argue with her, said goodbye to the few friends I had made and went home. This was March, April time 1960. Incidentally, one of the guys that was in my 5th form class who was to became a best mate followed me and some weeks later he took the entrance exam for the RN, passed, and was to join me at HMS Collingwood in August.

So, for about four months I found a job on a building site where I became the general dogsbody and tea boy. I would, as the title infers, become a tea boy where three times a day at 10:00, midday and at 15:00 I would make literally a bucket of tea in a white enamel bucket. I would also take orders for cigarettes, rolls, sandwiches, pies etc. from the local shop and generally fetch and carry as requested.

On 18th May 1960 I reached the grand old age of sixteen. Three months later on 30th August 1960 I joined the Navy. I was issued with a railway warrant and told to report to the RN recruiting office in Charing Cross Road, London, which I did with due diligence. I was, with a load more newly enlisted RN recruits, to be subjected to a severe medical exam parading around for a good hour or so in the nude having every orifice peered into before being told to dress, collect our belongings and then be taken to the station to get the train for Fareham in Hampshire, arriving late afternoon. A RN lorry was waiting for us to be taken to HMS Collingwood, which was soon to be christened 'Collingrad'. My life in the Royal Navy had started.

Once at Collingwood we were herded into a classroom and talked at by several people. We met our instructor. The time was getting towards 1600 so we were taken to the New Entry Division dining hall where we were treated to 'tea' Royal Naval style: a mug of what we always were led to believe was Bromide invested and a selection of small three-to-a-packet biscuits. There was also a selection of jam and bread. I was soon to learn quickly of some quaint English eating habits when a lad from Liverpool (Scouser) made a sugar sandwich whilst another lad from Newcastle (Geordie) selected a packet of rich tea biscuits, buttered two slices of bread, dunked his biscuits in his tea and spread the biscuits between his two slices of buttered bread.

We were taken to our mess; a long wooden hut on stilts with the similar huts either side. There were about ten huts in total, connected at one end by a corridor leading to a bathroom and toilets or 'heads' as they were to be called. After being taken to the bedding store to draw some bedding we went back to our mess and basically left to get on with getting to know each other.

This was our last night, if you could call it that, of freedom. We were the second to last entry to do New Entry training at HMS Collingwood. Our class had Sick Bay Attendants (SBAs), Direct Entry Mechanicians and us Greenies or Electrical Branch ratings both General Service and Fleet Air Arm.

The first day was a day of being talked at again, being taken to slops to draw our 'kit'; but first we were taken into a classroom and made to 'sign on', but not before one of our number had decided he had seen enough of the RN and asked to leave. He was given a railway warrant and was never seen again.

Training began. We spent a lot of the first days getting our kit sorted, learning how to mark each item with a wooden type made up with your name, some black or white paint and every item of kit had to be marked somewhere invisible to the eye with your name. Not me; I managed to stamp the back of my blue suits with my name then spent hours trying to remove the cock up. Interspersed with learning how to march, salute, stand still without talking; when not doing that a whole lot of instructional films on all the social disease known to man and how to avoid them, knot tying, how to sail a whaler etc. etc. all good stuff, useful in future life in the RN.

Towards the end of our first six weeks we were taken to HMS St Vincent for the day to do a series of swimming tests and to climb the mast. Yea right, I said no way was I going up there and I didn't. Our instructor was a three badge PO Gunnery instructor. He was a true gent, obviously served somewhere in the Second World War and albeit firm he was definitely fair. I think if it weren't for him, I wouldn't have survived the first six weeks. He saw I was bricking climbing the mast and told me to get to the Devil's elbow across and back down the other side but I had my own plan I climbed part way up and mingled with them coming down and descended without being seen... phew, thank God for that!

We passed out fully trained in the art of marching, firing and chucking an Enfield 303 RN issue rifle about. The Part 2 training was to commence which meant back to school for six weeks learning how to become an Electrical Mechanic, back then we were called Electricians Mate, but before that we were taken to see the PSO, or Personal Selections Officer, who was a Blue Badge Officer or WREN Officer.

She interviewed us individually and asked us what we wanted to be within the Electrical Branch. We had four choices, EM, REM, EM(A) or REM(A) or Electrical Mechanic, Radio Electrical Mechanic, Electrical Mechanic (Air) or Radio Electrical Mechanic (Air). I said I'd like to be a REM please, she said they had enough REMs for the time being, but I could become a REM(A) if I wanted. I said no thanks and if I wanted to play with aeroplanes I would have joined the RAF. Well that went down like a lead fart, was told not to be so rude and given the title of Junior Electrical Mechanic 2nd Class.

Albert Calland

When this incident occurred, I was serving in *Ark Royal* in Devonport, I was a stoker (MEM1).

I joined in September 1964 at Ganges, followed by a diesel course at Sultan. My first ship was *Llandaff* 1966-67 Devonport then work up at Portland followed by Far East then *Nurton* based at Lochinvar South Queensferry. I followed this by a spell ashore at the grandly named Royal Naval School of Hydrographical Survey, where as a 20 year old I had to learn to cook a hot two course lunch for up to eight matelots on a primus stove cooker daily. I grew up very quickly that draft. This was followed by the *Ark Royal* 1969-72, then *Bulldog* 1972-75 and finally ship's company in Fisgard until discharge in early 1976.

I skipped through the dockyard one summer evening in 1971. I had a date, the first for quite a while and while she wasn't a page three model she was a good looking girl and she was around my age, which for me was rather unusual! Little did I know then this was the prelude to one of the most bizarre sexual encounters of my then young but experienced life.
      We had met while waiting in a long taxi queue, started chatting, shared a cab and agreed to meet at seven on the following Friday. I couldn't wait. The Dockyard police officer looked me up and down in the normal manner wondering if I could be smuggling cigarettes but thankfully let me go unhindered and I made my way to the local bus stop where we had arranged to meet, I would have preferred the pub.
      Well I waited and waited and lo and behold I had been stood up again. Bollocks thought I and made my way to the Avondale boozer just outside the Dockyard

gate to consider what to do next. After a couple I decided to hop on a bus and make my way up town for the evening so I drank up and made my way to the bus stop and waited; this was when things took a very bizarre turn.

While waiting, a little blue invalid carriage drove past with a young woman at the wheel. She smiled, went past then returned driving the other way, smiled again and repeated this a few times then made a gesture to walk further down the road where she was waiting in a side street. At this point she beckoned me into her strange vehicle. As I had sipped a few cans of Dutch courage before coming ashore and had a few in the pub I thought why not.

She gestured to me to get in the car, people of a certain age will realise how difficult that was. Anyway I squeezed in and sat on the battery pack which I was later to discover was not a good idea if you are wearing crimplene trousers, or maybe any trousers where battery acid is implicated. We started to talk, and one thing naturally led to another which in the confines of the little blue plastic machine would have been difficult enough, but what I haven't mentioned was that when I got in the car I discovered that my new friend came complete with callipers on one leg.

Passion being what passion is, we managed to manoeuvre enough to enable the deed to continue. Now, I am not one to think too deeply at times like that, but it suddenly occurred to me that if we managed accidentally to achieve a position where her callipers shorted the battery terminals there would be one hell of a flash and she would weld herself to the battery. I have been in some situations where for one reason or another ardour has been curtailed for one reason or another, but as that thought crossed my mind all passionate thoughts disappeared and all I could think of was standing at the side of the road trying to chisel the poor girl free from her very large batteries.

It was at that moment that I had to curtail any further activity, embarrassingly make my excuses, say a curt good night and to be frank "do a runner". I made my way solemnly back to the pub, had a couple of drinks, popped next door to the chippy, bought supper and made my way back onboard. As I crossed the gangway the Quartermaster shouted with extreme mirth, "Hey stoker, do you realise you are showing your bare arse?" It was then I saw that leaking battery acid had dissolved my crimplene trousers and some of my boxers and that I must have been stood at the bar in the boozer and in the chippy with my trousers slowly melting away!

Avondale Arms, Plymouth

After another incident, on board the *Bulldog* in 1972-75, myself and the jimmy didn't get on at all. I won't name anyone but he was quite old school; always wore full suit and tie at sea which was very strange on a survey ship. We were surveying off Islay in the Western Isles when I heard the pipe 'standby to hoist *Wake* (the seven ton motor survey boat) to the gunwale', a quick job while we shifted position on the survey ground where we would lower again. The downside of this for me, as day work stoker and tanky, was I would have to transfer water from stbd. to port to compensate for the boat's weight and keep the ship upright. Well as soon as I heard the pipe off I went and began, then returned to the dining hall, made myself a coffee and waited for the boat to hoist and the ship to come upright.

Once the boat was on board the boats crew and the hoisting crew also came into the dining hall for a wet and a break. That's when the Jimmy, quite irate, burst in and started on me, "Why aren't you getting the ship upright, why are you sat here?"

This in a full dining room. I calmly explained that I was transferring water from stbd. to port, that we had two fifty ton tanks and that we had less than fifty tons of water remaining so I couldn't spill any, and there was a datum mark on the forward bulkhead to which I had masking taped a nut on a piece of line to act as a plumb bob so I knew when we were upright. When I explained this he turned quite purple slammed the sliding door and we weren't the best of friends again.

Harry and Michael Milne
Father and Son in the RN

I come from a naval family; my paternal grandfather was a PO shipwright and my maternal grandfather was a dockyard matey in Devonport Dockyard. My father was a marine engineer in the Royal Navy, initially as an ERA (Engineer Room Artificer) and then, as an MEO (Marine Engineer Officer). To cap it all, my mother joined the WRNS (Women's Royal Naval Service) during WWII, but was medically discharged in 1944. She always blamed her discharge on me, which I could never understand, as I wasn't born until 1945.

My Father, Harry Milne

My father joined the RN in 1938, just before his 16th birthday, as an artificer apprentice, or boy 'tiff. Artificers were the RN's skilled craftsmen, across a wide range of trades. He served throughout WWII and, in 1942, was on a battleship, *HMS Howe*, on Arctic Convoys. They were based in Scapa Flow and escorted convoys to

68

Murmansk and Archangel, battling not only U-boats, dive bombers and surface raiders, but also the appalling weather - gale force winds and monster waves and a build-up of ice on the upper deck, which had to be chipped off daily to avoid capsizing. Arctic Convoys were described by Winston Churchill as "The worst journey in the world". Later, in 1944, he was on a cruiser, *HMS Diadem*, off the Normandy coast for the D-Day landings. In the whole time that I knew him, he never said very much about his experiences during WWII, although he had a host of other stories (most of them very funny) about the rest of his time in the RN. It was my mother, who told me that while he was on Arctic Convoys, he lost 3 stone (42 pounds) in weight, mainly due to spending long hours in the engine room in very hot and humid conditions and then going onto the upper deck, for some fresh air, where it was well below freezing.

Promoted to Commissioned Officer

In 1955, my father was promoted to SD (Special Duties) Officer, with the rank of Acting Commissioned Engineer Officer and one thin gold ring, like a Lieutenant Commander's middle ring. These are his official promotion photos; note the black cap and gloves in the photo on the left. He was wearing gloves because the previous year he was involved in an explosion in the ship's fridges on *HMS*

Launceston Castle, which resulted in third degree burns to his hands and needed an extensive skin graft on the back of one hand. You can just about make out the severe scarring in the photo on the right in mess undress. For the remainder of his life, he always felt the cold in his hands and could accurately predict snowfall.

***HMS Eagle* in Malta**
In 1956, my father was appointed to *HMS Eagle*, which was stationed in Malta. At some point, Prince Philip, who by then was a senior admiral in the RN, was due to conduct an official inspection of *HMS Eagle*. Before he came onboard, there was a problem with the sirens on *Eagle* and my father, who was responsible for them, had some of his team working to repair the problem. When Prince Philip came onboard in Grand Harbour, there was a full side party waiting to greet him i.e. Bosun's calls, junior & senior rates and various officers, including the XO and CO, all in No 1s, waiting to pipe him aboard. Just as he came to the top of the companionway and the side party was about to pipe him aboard, one of the sirens malfunctioned and emitted a very loud deep blast (just imagine what the sirens on an aircraft carrier sound like!). There was immediate panic from the side party "Who the hell was responsible for

that?" asked the CO, but of course, nobody could provide an answer.

The incident passed over and Prince Philip was taken off on an inspection tour of the ship, ending up in the wardroom, where all the ship's officers were waiting to be introduced to him. They were lined up in strict order of rank, with the Commanders at the one end and my poor old Dad, with his one thin ring, at the other end. After some time, Philip reached my father and the CO introduced him. Philip asked my father what he was responsible for, to which he replied, "I look after the steam catapults, the refrigeration plant and (hum) the sirens, sir". Philip said, "Were you responsible for that god-awful noise when I came onboard?" and my father replied, somewhat sheepishly "Yes sir, I was". Philip leaned in very close and whispered to my father, "You're the only person to have got away with farting at me in public!". My father dined out on that story for many years after that and, although it was considered too risqué for my delicate ears at the time, I have heard it many times, when I was older.

The photo shows my father, on the flight deck of *HMS Eagle* and you can clearly see where I get my good looks from!

Family Life in Malta

In 1958, my father was appointed to the heavy repair ship, *HMS Ausonia*, in Malta. She was berthed in Lazaretto Creek and he was running a team carrying out maintenance and repairs on the destroyers in Sliema Creek. It was an accompanied posting, so my mother and I joined him and spent two and a half years there. I went to the RN School Tal-Handaq, outside the village of Qormi and not far from Luqa Airport. The school was the fore-runner of a modern comprehensive school with both grammar and secondary modern elements, but there wasn't a boundary between them. Every term, based on the end of term exam results, they operated a relegation and demotion system, rather like the English football leagues, where the top two in each form went up and the bottom two went down. This system worked remarkably well and kept everyone on their toes. Indeed, I knew several people who were promoted from a top secondary modern form to a bottom grammar form and did very well in their 'O' Levels. The other surprise was that it was co-educational. Coming from a single-sex school, the presence of these strange creatures, with bumps under their jerseys was a complete revelation to me. Up to that stage, I'd been rather studious and only interested in building model aeroplanes. For some strange reason, I lost interest in model aeroplanes around that time.

The other thing that Malta did was to expose me to the RN in a way that I'd never been before. Most Sundays, during the summer, we used to take an MFV (motor fishing vessel) from *Ausonia* to the Blue Lagoon, which is part of the island of Comino, in the channel between Malta and Gozo. We would anchor in the Blue Lagoon, drop the drinks overboard in a weighted bag to keep cool and spend the rest of the day swimming and sunbathing. I grew to appreciate the lifestyle and even went to sea on *Ausonia* for a week's exercise around the Greek islands. I guess this probably sowed the seeds which germinated later. My father's appointment was extended by six months, to allow me to sit my 'O' Levels and we returned to the UK in 1961.

'A' Levels and University
Back in the UK, I re-joined my old school, in the sixth form. I did maths and science for my 'A' levels and then

decided to do an electrical engineering degree at Bristol University. In my final year at university, it suddenly dawned on me that I would need to decide what career I wanted to pursue and, to avoid getting a real job, I decided to join the RN on a short service commission.

As an aside, I was advised to join the local RNR, to get some idea of what I was letting myself in for and, for a short while, I wore square rig on *HMS Flying Fox*, as an Upper Yardsman – note the white flash on my sleeve. This experience convinced me that square rig was far too uncomfortable and scratchy for me and that fore and aft rig was much more to my taste.

Before I graduated, I applied to join the RN and was sent to the Admiralty Interview Board in Gosport. This was the most demanding interview process that I've ever been through in my entire career. It takes place over two days and includes exercises in the pool and gym. You are constantly assessed for your leadership skills and potential, even during off-duty occasions, such as meals.

After being accepted by the RN, I was invited to spend a week at the RN Engineering College, Manadon before officially joining. We went onboard a number of ships and visited the Royal Marine Commando Training Centre at Lympstone and RNAS Culdrose. Before the visit to Culdrose, we were instructed not to wear any synthetic clothing, because we were going up in a helicopter and synthetic materials are highly inflammable. When we were putting on flying overalls, they noticed that one member of our group was wearing a nylon shirt, which he had to remove. To keep him warm, the pilot offered him his No 1 Flying Suit, with gold badges etc.

Once we were airborne, we were fascinated with the views over the Lizard Peninsula until the pilot decided to play that trick where they hover at a reasonable height and then feather the blades, so that the helicopter drops like a stone, before engaging the blades again and retaining altitude. He repeated this a number of times until our stomachs were thoroughly churned up and on the last drop we could hear the unmistakable sound of somebody being thoroughly sick, all over the pilot's No 1 Flying Suit!

Initial Training in the RN
After I graduated, in 1966, I joined the RN as an Electrical Officer on the Supplementary List and was sent my joining instructions for Victory Barracks in Portsmouth, along with a voucher to obtain my uniform suits from an 'approved tailor'. Luckily, my father knew the drill and strongly suggested that I go to Gieves, who knew exactly what was required. Some in my joining class went to other tailors, such as Burton's, with disastrous results. When I arrived at Victory Barracks, the first thing that happened was that we were issued with the remainder of our kit - shirts, ties, caps, shoes, socks etc. The first time that we formed up on the parade ground in full rig and were inspected was an eye-opener, particularly for the people that had been to Burton's!

We then had to learn some basic rudiments of drill, saluting, marching etc, which wasn't helped by the fact that our drill instructor was a Chief GI (Chief Gunnery

Instructor) who was being invalided out of the RN because he had laryngitis. You can't imagine the confusion caused by a Chief GI, whose sole function in life is to shout orders, without a voice! At one point, we almost marched into a brick wall, until one bright spark had the common sense to shout "squad, about turn".

The other part of our training was known as a 'knife & fork course', where we learnt how to behave as an officer and a gentleman in the wardroom. One of the things that this involved was a mess dinner, which, despite the warnings my father had given me, was still quite an eye-opener. Mess dinners in the RN are very formal affairs, where everyone is expected to be on their best behaviour, until the port is passed and the loyal toast drunk, along with the speeches. After that, it descends rapidly into total mayhem, with all kinds of shenanigans. The following day, I was back at Gieves for some minor repairs to my mess undress jacket, when I saw another of my class asking if they could sew the arms back on his!

About a month after I joined, I received my first pay cheque. After several years of pecuniary university living, this went to my head and I marched out of the dockyard in full No 1's to the nearest bank and asked to speak with the manager to 'discuss my investments'. He was a very traditional bank manager, just like Captain Mainwaring in Dad's Army, who listened attentively to my request to invest £100. A few weeks later, I received a pass book for a building society with £100 invested in it. I kept that pass book for many years, as a reminder not to be such a pompous twit.

I was sent to HMS Collingwood, the RN electrical school to learn all about the electrical equipment which was then in service. My abiding memory of that was, after another mess dinner, taking one of my course-mates back to his cabin and stripping off his uniform and laying him on his bunk completely starkers to sleep it off. The routine in Collingwood at that time was that WRNS stewards would give you a shake at 0700 and place a cup of tea on your bedside cabinet. Apparently, he woke around 0800, to find about a dozen cups of stone cold tea on his cabinet - I leave you to work out how they got there!

This is a photo of my class in Collingwood. None of us are looking very great, because it was the morning after a memorable mess dinner. I was invited to Collingwood's 60th anniversary in 2000. What's really upset me was that after the official ceremonies and a suitably satisfying lunch, I was free to wander round and found a copy of my class photo ...... in the MUSEUM!!

Michael Milne

Harry Milne's Medals

78

Steve Mathis

As a child Steve Mathis had always had a love of ships. He had grown up in Portsmouth and for years had watched the warships slip out of harbour with their crews stood on the upper decks, returning after another amazing deployment, probably full of new stories, souvenirs and memories that would last a lifetime. He would scour the Portsmouth News every night for the shipping movements section so that he would know which ones were due back the following day, then he would skip school and go watch them sail past.

Steve had come from a long line of military families. His father had been in the Fleet Air Arm, his grandfather was a diver and three cousins were all out at sea on the *Grampus*, *Phoebe* and *Caprice*. He knew what he wanted to do and that was to travel as much as possible and what better way to do it than signing up for the Royal Navy!

"I had thought that if I didn't make the grade for the RN what other Armed Forces would I consider, the RM and RAF but not the Army. The bit I wasn't keen on with Land Forces was that when posted if you didn't like the place then you were stuffed."

On 4th August 1969, at just 16 years old, he stepped off the train at Plymouth station on a baking hot day to be met be a group of sailors that would escort them to their training camp. They all piled into the back of a Bedford Truck and were taken over to HMS Raleigh where they were put in old Nissen huts. He was very nervous; he didn't know what he was in for but he did know that this was the start of his adventures.

As the class of around 36 new joiners sat to read the contract and sign on the dotted line, three of them bottled it and went home. For Steve, his training had now begun.

Steve Mathis class of 1973 - Steve is back row, top left

He did two weeks training before he got his first wage, £3 in total, which consisted of a march in front of the Pay Office, salute and holding out of the pay book. After his part one training was completed he had to stay at Raleigh to continue his part two – seamanship. He had applied to be a Radar Plotter (RP) and one of his jobs would be to work the upper decks on a ship when coming into harbour, towing, replenishing and doing general maintenance. After he had learned all this it was back over to Portsmouth in order for him to learn his trade up on Portsdown Hill at HMS Dryad. It would be four more weeks of learning before finally he would be ready to join his first ship.

"I joined *Ark Royal* R09 in Guzz in April 1970. I wasn't sure, if my memory serves me correctly, but I was supposed to be drafted to *Danae* but it was cancelled and I ended up on the *Ark*. Captain Lygo was our Skipper."

He was taken down to his mess, 4Wa0 mess two decks under the after lift and once he had settled in he was given a part of ship – the Foretop and boats party. The first time he met his "Sea Dad" it was during a RAS (Replenishment at Sea).

"My Sea Dad I met in total darkness on the RAS Point, you couldn't see anyone's face only the light on their lifejacket."

The *Ark* held some good memories for Steve, on one occasion Peter Cook and Dudley Moore had a comedy programme called 'Not Only But Also' and on one episode they played the piano on a farewell song and at the very end a dummy was strapped to it before being fired off using one of the three catapults, much to everyone's amusement!

His job on board was working in the Operations Room on the RADAR plot when he was not on the upper deck conducting maintenance routines or doing general duties on board between decks. But his first run ashore left him with a different kind of memory.

As the ship was going into Rotterdam the accommodation ladder, made of solid oak, was being moved and two of them were told to go on the outboard side of the ladder and keep it from hitting the bulkheads as they used the block and tackles. Unfortunately, Steve didn't get his hand out of the way in time and it caught his finger and broke it! Not a good start to his first run!

But there would be many more great runs ashore after this. The *Ark Royal* would take him to Oslo, Malta,

Gibraltar, Palma Nova, Naples, Antigua, Freeport (Grand Bahama), St Thomas and the Virgin Islands.

Although it was always about the runs ashore, the ship always had some kind of drama to put her in the headlines. On 9th November 1970 the carrier was in the Mediterranean and being shadowed by a Russian Kotlin Class destroyer when the smaller ship suddenly cut across the bows of the carrier. The two warships collided and seven of the Russian crew went over the side, only five of them were picked up alive.

Another time they lost a Phantom aircraft in the English Channel but that was nothing compared to the shock of one of the aircraft handlers accidentally pushing a Buccaneer over the side!

While in Malta the side party got to work on the maintenance of the side of the ship and got a roasting themselves when it was found that "Ban the Bomb" had been painted down the side of the ship in red lead paint.

One of the most high-profile visits for the *Ark Royal* while Steve was on board was New York City… a place where a British aircraft carrier would be most welcome and the delight reciprocated. The carrier anchored to a buoy and the ship's boats were being used to ferry crew members ashore as well as the liberty boat.

The ships' fast motor launch (FML) was let go and Steve was the bowman taking personnel to the jetty. They would depart from the quarterdeck and head off slowly, opening up the throttles once they had cleared the ship. However, on this occasion they almost met with disaster as they hit floating ice bobbing around and it caused a hole to open up in the hull of the boat. Thankfully they were able to return safely, if not they would not have lasted more than three minutes in the freezing water that was 12 degrees below zero!

New York turned out to be a great place to be, although they were told not to go ashore in groups of less than five people due to the number of shootings and muggings that there had been there.

As the ship weighed anchor and headed back to the UK, they passed yachtsman Chay Blyth who was about to complete his mission to go around the world single handed. It was using the time at sea that Steve studied hard for his promotion exams, some of the questions were unbelievable but they have stuck with him even today – how heavy was the anchor (9 tons) and the links (80lbs each). He was all good with the seamanship but failed his core role due to him not doing any anti-submarine work (he had come top in the aircraft side of it!).

The *Ark* then went to Mayport Naval Yard in Florida and this is where Steve regales us with another incident that he was involved in.

"I owned a canoe and kept it on board, there were about twenty canoes on board. We lowered the boats from 3-deck on the carrier and then you just shimmied down a rope and climbed into it that way. It was not easy and a lot fell in! We paddled across the river to the surf beach at Jacksonville where we tried out the Yanks surfboards and they tried our canoes. But coming back to the ship, we were met by a huge US Navy Launch who told us the Dockyard was a 'No Go' area. The leader of our group had to tell him we were off the Carrier!"

Another time on that same trip the carrier was "cruising round in a box waiting for daylight and to drop the pick (anchor) off St Thomas Virgin Is, this bloke legged it over the side during the middle watch and took a lifejacket with him and a canoe! We could see the lights ashore, but distance is deceptive at sea and the Lifebuoy

Ghost saw him during the morning watch, he had drifted out to sea instead of towards land."

The sailor was promptly rescued and ended up at DQ's (Detention Quarters – military prison).

HMS Ark Royal (photo by Hugh Llewelyn)

After around two years on board the *Ark Royal*, Steve left her in the summer of 1972 where he was given a choice of two drafts – the aircraft carrier *Hermes* or the *Keppel*. He chose the *Keppel* but then had to check out Janes Fighting Ships at the library to find out what sort of a ship it was. Turned out it was a Blackwood Class Type 14 Frigate built in 1945.

Looking back, it was his time on both *Dido* and *Juno* that leave him with the fondest memories. "They were my best ships," he said. "78 was the best deployment I ever did, I was on Juno, (AKA the Raving J) part of the 5th Frigate Squadron, *Blake* was I/C of the Group. *Birmingham* left Pompey late and we as Canteen

Boat had to wait for her. We were tasked on *Juno* to patrol off Tortola and they flew a RM Major out to train the Internal Security Platoon which I was in."

The island was a British ruled island and trouble was brewing. A black man had been killing white women on the island and he was waiting to have his sentence passed down, but riots were kicking off and so a team was prepared on *Juno* to stand by to land. "We were fully booted and spurred in You-Can't-See-Me-Suits for 36hrs... but nothing came of it so we had to wait for *Birmingham* to join the group and we transited the Panama together."

Steve Mathis

The rest of the trip was nothing short of an amazing adventure for Steve and his shipmates. A stop in Brest (France), Bermuda, Belize, four weeks Annual Maintenance Period in San Diego (California), one week in Long Beach, one week in Victoria BC - the rest of the group went to Esquimalt Navy Yard as they had done the Tortola stint they were in the city – "from Victoria to Prince Rupert British Columbia where I trapped an Indian when we were on Black Russians I nicked her hat and threw it in the sea and my mates kept telling me she was out to kill me!"

Then it was Prince Rupert to San Francisco for a week, then Acapulco for a week, through the Panama, one week in San Juan Puerto Rico, a week in Dominica for their Independence Day, three days in Key West (Florida), two days Banyan in St Thomas (US Virgin Islands) then home for Christmas leave before heading back out to the Med for three months. He left the *Juno* in 1980.

By now he had been on board six ships and so he was sent to the shore base HMS Raleigh and loaned to HMS Dryad so he could complete a Radar Conversion Course ADAWS5. But by now he had other things on his mind. "My Mum sadly passed away at 47 and I totally switched off."

That same year he was back at sea when he was drafted to the Leander class frigate *Arethusa*, but it was on here that he had a brush with the military law in an act of self-defence that would change his career path.

While he was Dining Hall Party one of the PO stokers didn't take too much of a liking to Steve and decided to bully him at every opportunity. "He was always on my case," he would recall, with incidents occurring far too often to the point of him hating his time on board this ship.

So the ship was doing the Submarine Captain's qualifying course off Scotland and the ship went alongside on completion. Steve went out with the lads as was usual and had been drinking McEwan's Export on draught all afternoon and generally winding down from the stress of being on board. But once again his nemesis decided to give him grief and, after having enough drinks to square up to him, threatened to "knock ten bells of s*** out of him."

The Petty Officer went back to the ship where he waited for him, knowing he had consumed alcohol and that he was vulnerable. Having another go at him he once again lashed out and threatened to drop him... but this time the PO had witnesses who testified against him when he was put on a charge. He was found guilty and lost both of his good conduct badges and given 60 days 2nd Class – which was 60 days punishment: 48 days of No 9's followed by 12 days of No 10s. His next run ashore he would have to be escorted by the Leading Hand of the mess.

But it was not just this incident that led to it being an unhappy ship for Steve. "Basically on *Arethusa* it was the only ship out of the seven (that I served on) where there were rumblings of a mutiny... we had a Junior Skipper out to win prizes and so we stayed in Guzz during the week and put to sea every weekend, so only the ones living local could get home. Halfway through that draft the skipper changed and it got better."

But unfortunately, this draft left a bitter taste and he was no longer enjoying his career. "I was getting anxious because I felt the only thing the mob was teaching me was how to drink. After getting 2nd class (punishment) it just became a job and not the adventure - I hardly ever drink now"

He then made a decision that would put an end to everything and decided to leave the navy. "I was given two choices by who was to be my wife. 1, come out and get married or 2, stop in and complete 22 years. The 2nd Class punishment didn't help and I was getting anxious that at 40, which would have been 8 years on, that I would be a 40 year old schoolboy with a pension."

Weighing up the pro's and cons he finally walked out of the gates of HMS Nelson on 19th January 1984. He had served on seven ships, on each one he would buy a souvenir Zippo lighter for his father, a tradition he kept up throughout his time in the Navy. In 14 years he had visited

33 countries and left at the rank of AB but had partially passed for Leading Hand should he want to pursue it and stay in.

Looking back on some of the events of those years, Steve recalls a few incidents that not many people will have heard of, let alone remember.

"Chatham was different from all the other harbours, the RN use it as it was in a non-tidal basin. *Keppel* was based there as was *Dido* and *Juno* although after their refits they went to Pompey. If you wanted the heads you had to use the shore side heads. At night before Pipe Down the Duty Watch Seaman would put out four large stainless steel dustbins, the Juniors got the short straw as the AB's put out the bins, 1 fwd, 2 midships and 1 aft. The idea being that if you needed to go you could p*** in the bin. At Call the Hands the Juniors would empty the bins shore side, most of it used to go down the scuppers. We had a sprog straight out of training. If you have seen pictures of the Leander Class Frigates, they had a large towed array on the back end that was the 199 Well. Most people would go up the ladder with the bin behind them, the sprog decided to take it up in front of him, when he got to the top rung, he lost his balance and the lot came down on him.

"Another thing that happened I can't remember if it were on the *Dido* or *Juno*, we hid all the dockies tea pots and they threatened to walk out on strike unless they turned up.

"On *HMS Fawn*, a ship that was painted white instead of grey and had a top speed of 14 knots, the Skipper wanted us to do a board and search off Milford Haven, so we launched the Gemini (boat)... but as they boarded the trawler took off with the Gemini Crew onboard!

"Another thing on *Fawn*... we were creating charts from Milford Haven to Wexford in Southern Ireland and the Gemini crew had to put up a marker to line the computers up. As it was January and freezing cold they lit a fire, however it burnt the whole Island down which turned out to be a bird sanctuary!"

So lots of dits to spin after 14 years, some great runs, even better runs ashore and even time based foreign. "The longest I ever spent anywhere was five months in Gib and I loved it."

Asked if he still keeps in touch with anybody today, he is fondly still following the fleet and watching the ships come into port.

"As for keeping in touch with the lads, I went to one *Ark Royal* Reunion in the S/R's mess in Drake, a *Dido* one which was very well organized as it was all weekend and included the families, and two *Arethusa* ones, the first one was All Commissions and my mate and I left early as we didn't know anyone, the second one, I organized and I was talking to 72 members of the 80 - 83 commission, 36 were going, it was to be in Guzz as we were Guzz based, 6 turned up and I called the rest a bunch of "Shoot Through's" and they said I was a w**ker which I can live with.

"A PO I knew, he is still alive and we met him and his wife in Guzz, another Ex *Arethusa* who is 15 years younger than me, and my old run ashore oppo; we met up in 2018 after not seeing each other since 1975. He was with his wife and I took my good lady, then we vowed not to wait that long again so we met up in Pompey last year.

"After I left I did a bit of Security Work in schools/building sites, Industrial Cleaning in Rover Cars at Longbridge then on the tracks/car finishing lines working on the old Mini and Metro putting items on new cars every three minutes. I did ten years there and then transferred to Land Rover in Solihull working on the Land Rover 90/120 and Army Wolf, the Range Rover and Freelander for two years then took my voluntary redundancy."

Asked if he regretted leaving the navy when he did... Steve replied with one simple answer.

"Yes!"

Ellen Turner

My name is Ellen and I applied to join the QARNNS when I was 16, was accepted and commenced training in October 1975, aged 18.

I had never ever wanted to do anything other than nurse, this being my vocation, and I wanted to join the RN. My Maternal Grandfather was a river pilot in the Merchant Navy, he died before I was born but I wanted to follow in his footsteps.

I wanted the opportunity of travelling and also the uniform, which a proper nurse used to wear, not the supermarket overalls they wear today.

So in October I left my hometown of Bristol arriving at RNH Stonehouse, where I was finally left by my parents to join all the other members of my class.

We were taken, in a group, to be shown our nurses quarters. Each one of us were in a room of four, the total number of the group at the start were thirteen.

We were given a guided tour and shown all the places around the hospital where all our facilities would be found.

So we as a group got to know each other and spoke of our backgrounds and why we decided to join the QARNNS. Most of the girls wanted to join because they came from a very large family, which I was quite envious of as I was an only child; I had tons of friends but lacked the freedom most of them had due to a strict mother.

So we had all unpacked in our new rooms and had eaten, we didn't realise that it was a nightly thing that we were all checked as *in* our beds by 2200. Actually, checked bed by bed by a torch by the PO Wren, of the nurses quarters!

However after a while we sorted this by packing a couple of beds to make it look as though we were in them, then a sheet tied hung from the sash window as we slid down in turn and escaped into Plymouth.

We did our six weeks training, passed, were given our nursing buckles after six months on a red belt. We were shown all the wards and we were given our individual wards that we were training on. We were then shown the wards that we would be working on, when we were out of school. The hours were Early 7am to 1pm, Late 1pm to 8pm and Night 8pm to 7am. The nights came every six weeks and were twelve hours per night for fourteen nights on the trot. Our accommodation on nights were all sleeping within two rooms specifically for nights with dark curtains.

Our social life was very good. Groups of us would go down union street in the evenings, drink and smoke a little too much arriving back at very late hours, only to have to get up two hours later and be transported to various geriatric hospitals in Plymouth to do our care of the elderly training. The NHS nurses didn't like us at all, I think because we had very proper uniform.

We had to make our hats ourselves and they had to be spray starched as firm as possible, then we would fold them as instructed. Luckily our dresses and aprons were done for us.

We had four rail warrants a year and after doing our fourteen nights we were given seven days night duty standoff then take one weeks annual leave to make it two weeks.

In 1977 I qualified as a SEN (State Enrolled Nurse) after two years training. I always wanted to be a bedside nurse SRN (State Registered Nurse), which took three years training and you were management on qualification.

So shortly after qualifying I was drafted to RNAS Culdrose for six months where we were responsible for all medical care of all ranks, suturing, plastering, bandaging and generally looking after the sick.

My next draft was to HMS Drake, working in the sick bay and when on call, going to the frigates to attend. We would work duty weekends from Friday afternoon till Monday morning.

I was then drafted to RM Stonehouse Barracks, which was coincidental as I had been going out with a Royal Marine for a while. I married him in 1979 and we were given a house in St Budeaux, opposite the Tamar ferry, where I met many more friends around the married quarters. To get into work from there we each bought a bike.

We were the very first group of QARNNS to go to Norway with the marines and run a sick bay, we went in January for ten weeks.

After a while my husband and I talked; I wanted to leave the navy purely because I clobbered every weekend whilst he was off, his rota nearly always opposite mine. I always remember the commanding officer sending for me and stressing how I shouldn't leave, that he could send me to CTC Lympstone for draft as my then husband was going.

So it was later that year I went to HMS Drake with my suitcase and all my uniform, as we had to hand it all back (I really wish I'd kept my nursing cape).

What I failed to know, which the Commander was trying to tell me, was that my husband was playing around. After leaving Plymouth we moved to Exmouth then thank God got a married quarter in Honiton. It was here we bought our first house and three months after moving in he did a FO.

Keith Cooper

Neptune 1976

As my 12 years was coming to an end I was drafted to Neptune for my last year as PO of the gate. Early on I was summoned to the Commander's office to be advised that on no account was Prince Charles to be stopped and his ID checked when driving his Landy. Because of the Irish problem his vehicle would have no markings identifying whose car it was. I would only know it was the Prince by the number plate which was VGP 001. I smiled at this information and was demanded by the CO what I found so funny about this information. I had to explain that the plate to me said "Very Good Prince number 1" sir. Whereupon the CO let out a giggle and said to his minions that he thought that the Prince had a sense of humour. None of them had realised it 'till I pointed it out to them.

     Later on, because the gate staff were on shifts, I used to drive a Helensburgh taxi on off weeks. One of the other drivers was a smart arsed uni student who was amused by the term "need to know" and thought it a load of bollocks. He decided one night to grill a couple of sun dodgers about where they had been, how long, how deep they went, if they had nukes etc. He kept at it with the response of course being "need to know". When his passengers got to Helensburgh, they immediately rang the Commonwealth Police who manned the gate into the Purple area. No sooner did smarty pants get back to the main gate to wait for his next fare than he was suddenly surrounded by black unmarked cars, hauled out of his taxi and whisked off to Glasgow where he spent the night. Very shaken the next day he related that the empty room with a small table, two chairs and a bright light in his face as per the movies was absolutely true. He never asked another sun dodger any more questions after that. He was a much chastened young man from then on.

I made the terrible mistake one day of waving through a two ringer, saluting him as he went through. Ten minutes later "Petty Officer Cooper, Commander's office at the rush". Oh shit, what have I done? I was met by a seriously pissed off Commander accompanied by the two ringer I had waved through without stopping him and checking his ID. I received a severe bollocking and advised in no uncertain terms that if I didn't do my gate duty by the book the fuckin book would be thrown at me. So!!!!! I spent the next night shift studying the "book" and was quite enlightened by what it contained with regard to procedures about admittance to the base.

Next morning I had my junior rate close half the gate and check all passes and ID's which meant stopping buses and looking at all civvy passes and sending them in to the gatehouse for telephone certification of who they were with the department they worked in. An escort would then have to be arranged to get them to their place of work. The milkman was turned around, also the baker who thought I had gone nuts.

Eventually the traffic was backed up all the way to Helensburgh, as I found out when the CO arrived under police escort to find out what was going on at the base. I would have been within my rights to request he remove himself from the gate as he got his baton out, opened the other half of the gate waving all and sundry through but I'd had my fun and didn't want to push my luck. He of course could do nothing about the fiasco as it was all in his precious book and he left me alone after that!

Simon Bloomfield

Simon joined the Navy in 1976 and by August he had joined the aircraft carrier *Ark Royal* as a stoker. His first day at sea was spent at emergency stations as the ship had a major fire on board. Worry set in as two of the lads he had joined up with were missing down in the area where the fire was raging, incredibly they were found at a different part of the ship completely oblivious of anybody looking for them – in the NAAFI queue!

Leaving the *Ark*, he was drafted to Chatham to the Craft Support Unit, looking after the survey vessels, but it was not long until he was back on another ship, this time *HMS Leander*. The lead frigate of her class, Simon was to join her in San Diego sat on a long haul flight with both Chinese laundrymen, one either side of him on the plane.

Finally joining the ship in Long Beach, the memories of this draft centred around the fact she always seemed to break down. For example, in Vancouver Island the stokers were waiting for a new blower to be delivered and the ship was alongside for around a week while this part arrived. When it finally landed at the dockyard the Canadian dockies opened it to reveal... parts of a combined harvester!

One time the ship was transiting under the famous Golden Gate Bridge in San Francisco and the bridge had to be closed off due to a threat of IRA supporters throwing green paint onto the ship as it passed underneath.

By 1981 he was a Leading Stoker and was enjoying a year shore-side at Chatham FMG, this time looking after the frigates. But it was soon time for him to join another frigate himself, one that would make headlines for all the wrong reasons.

HMS Antelope 1982 (Photo Dmgerrard)

He was to join *HMS Antelope* and it was soon heading towards the South Atlantic after the Argentine invasion of the Falkland Islands had seen a fleet of 101 ships sent off to retake the land. For this part, Simon has written a diary of events -

Falklands Diary
4th April 1982
I was serving on *HMS Antelope* as a Leading Marine Engineering Mechanic and the ship was berthed at Portland Naval Base being put through what's called a ship's workup. This is to test the ability of the ship in all scenarios including war, dealing with riots, disaster assistance and general operations.

The captain informed us that we would be sailing to Plymouth and storing the ship in preparation to sail to The Falkland Islands which has just been invaded by Argentina. We arrived later that day and everything we required was waiting on the jetty for us. Food, drink, machinery spares, you name it they got it. That night those who were not duty hit the streets of Plymouth on a massive drinking session.

5th April
We set sail for what we all thought was just government action to scare Argentina. On our way down we stopped at Ascension Island and had navy divers inspect the hull of the ship as the water was getting into the fuel. What they found was that the divers who did a welding repair in Plymouth had burned through the hull and made a hole in the fuel tank. Luckily it was full otherwise God knows what would have happened.

Once that was fixed we sailed, but halfway to the Falklands, we were told we had to take Captain Astiz of the Argentine Navy and a few members of the British Antarctic survey team back to Ascension Island. They had been brought north on a navy supply vessel that was needed more than us in the war zone. Captain Astiz was wanted by both France and Sweden for the murder of some of their citizens and was known as the blonde angel of death as he was involved in the interrogation and torture of political prisoners in Argentina during its 'dirty war' in the late 70s to early 80s.

Once we dropped these guys off, we turned around and headed back south again.

4th May
The day we realised how serious things were. The Captain informed the ship's company over the tannoy

system that an Exocet missile had hit *HMS Sheffield* and the ship had been abandoned. My first thoughts, and everyone else on board, were this is now serious and Argentina won't back down.

As we headed south, we could see Vulcan bombers overhead going for the Falklands to bomb the airfield. One day suddenly a large crate was dropped by parachute at low level from a Hercules aircraft that we had to retrieve; it was marked WO Smith SAS. More about this crate later!

22nd May
HMS Antelope arrived at The Falklands total exclusion zone. This was a zone where if any Argentine ships went inside they would be considered a threat and attacked. The following day we were tasked to sail into St Carlos water and stay at the entrance to perform air defence duties. Pretty stupid as we were not very well equipped for that role.

23rd May
Early that afternoon we were attacked by four Argentine Sky Hawks, and this is the story of what happened to me from that day through till after I was safely home.

I was in charge of the forward machinery space with one other marine engineer. This compartment contained two diesel generators and other auxiliary machinery. Our lunch had just been brought down by another crew member when over the ships tannoy we heard air raid warning red. Basically, prepare to be attacked. A few minutes later I felt two huge thuds and then we were informed we had been hit by two bombs; both happened to be just above the compartment we were stationed in.

These obviously caused damage to a lot of the ship's systems and even one of the diesel generators in our machinery space tripped (stopped).

The ship turned massively to the right, but in a panic, I said to the guys with me "let's get out of here!" as I thought the ship was listing. As we reached the hatch, the ship straightened up, and we went back down the ladder to await any instructions.

One of the bombs went through the side of the ship and through a senior rates recreation space where a first aid party were based, the other landed in the air conditioning space, both just above our compartment.

As the first bomb went through the senior rates rec space, it struck a beer barrel (truth but you'll never see it mentioned) the beer barrel exploded and killed my mate Mark Stevens, a young steward. Mark was only 17 but used to come out with us to the pubs and lots of the girls we knew loved him as he was so young looking. Fortunately, he was the only one of our ship's company to die that day.

After a short time, we were told either to make our way to the front of the ship on the upper deck or to the flight deck. I went to the flight deck; it was so cold, so we all went into the helicopter hanger as fortunately the helicopter had been tasked on another duty.

The Captain then made a request to get two Royal Engineer Army bomb disposal guys onboard in an attempt to defuse the bombs. Sgt Jim Prescott and WO John Philips were detached to carry this out. Navy divers who would typically do it either refused or were too busy?

Nobody really knows the truth, but I would love to ask him why he wanted to get the bomb defused and didn't do what other ship's captains decided to do, and that was to sail their ships out of the total exclusion zone, go alongside a support vessel, get their specialists to cut a hole in the side of the ship and then throw the bomb into the sea.

I was stood at the back of the hanger with an anti-ship Sea Skua missile between my legs when suddenly there was an almighty explosion, one of the bombs they were trying to defuse had exploded killing Sgt Jim Prescott and injuring WO John Philips at their fourth attempt at trying to defuse it. Everyone's natural reaction to the explosion was to get out of the hanger. The 15-20 guys standing at the front could see all the shrapnel landing on the flight deck and luckily managed to hold everyone back until the shrapnel stopped falling.

Once we were all on the flight deck, we put our life jackets on in preparation that we may have to jump over the side of the ship. Suddenly the emergency hatch from the lower decks to the flight deck opened and the engineering officer and a chief mechanic brought John Philips out. I remember this so clearly, he was clutching his left arm saying, "I can't wait to tell my wife and kids about this".

He had been given morphine which did the job. They had made several attempts to blow the fuse on the bomb, but nothing appeared to have happened. Unknown to them, the device had a 28-second delay and exploded when John Phillips was preparing to inspect it. They were both standing just 30ft from the explosive when it went off. Jim was killed by a door that was blown off caused by the explosion.

I was fortunate to meet John and tell him what he said when he climbed up to the flight deck when we met at a reunion onboard the *QE2*. Cunard invited survivors of the three ships it brought back to the UK on the 25th anniversary.

Suddenly, after maybe fifteen mins, there were about thirty small boats from other navy ships in bomb alley coming towards us. One was a landing craft from *HMS Fearless* that usually lands troops and land Rovers etc. The coxswain, who was a Royal Marine, was explicitly told not to come alongside us as a ship on fire is dangerous. He did, and I'll never forget those guys, especially when you hear the last part of my story.

I was the first off, and my excuse was I was helping them to rig their firefighting hoses they had on the landing craft. As I was one of the most highly trained firefighters on the ship, I could make that excuse. Everyone then followed me. When it was full, and we were ready to head back to *HMS Fearless* the First Lieutenant, who's next down from the Captain, came to the flight deck, saw us and said, "The Captain hasn't given the order to abandon ship". He was greeted with a lot of 'f*** off's.

The ship was on fire, and no way would anything put it out. One Leading Hand who wasn't even in our branch, the ones who are the most trained in firefighting, decided to get a gas turbine fire pump from down the side of the ship with the assistance of a few of his other branch ratings. I question if he even had any idea of how to start it as we were the ones who maintained it and it is not easy as you have to throw a large hose over the side and then wind it up 'till the turbine ignites. In my view, this endangered others and something I personally would not have done.

Once the landing craft was full, we headed to *HMS Fearless* and were given beds for the night. One of the guys who was the same branch and rank as I gave me some overalls. He was also the engineer on the landing craft that rescued us and also knew me as he served on *Ark Royal* with me. Dusty Miller. Remember his name. It will come up later.

24th May

In the morning, we were told to make our way down to the tank deck and spend the day there. The ship was all closed down in preparation for more air raids. They came, and one 1000lb bomb landed on the *Fearless* but luckily bounced off the upper deck and into the sea. Where we were seated in the tank deck, there was a large crate which I recognised as it was the one dropped by parachute for us to take south for Warrant Officer Smith SAS, who was now based on *Fearless*.

We found out later we were meant to take the SAS on the operation and drop them off somewhere the previous night had we not been bombed. By us, in the tank deck, a guy was cleaning the mud and grass off his mortar launcher, and it was all over the deck. A young officer from our ship said, "I hope you are going to clear that up?" His reply was, "Of course I will, I'm taking it back to Hereford." What he was basically saying was 'mind your own business, Sir, I'm in the SAS.'

The night of the 24th we were taken by boat across San Carlos Bay to *MV Norland* a North Sea ferry and sailed for South Georgia. Think it took a few days and once we were there, we transferred to the *QE2* and sailed for home. Survivors of *HMS Ardent* and *HMS Coventry* were also onboard, some showing signs of burns, including the Captain of the *Coventry* who happens to be the comedian Miranda Hart's dad. His forehead was severely burnt, but there were others from those ships who were a lot worse, and we're still on the hospital ships.

11th June

After a few weeks of utter boredom, we arrived in the Solent and we're all told to get on the upper deck in preparation for arrival in Southampton where our families were waiting. I saw this lifeboat with Yarmouth Lifeboat written on the side and thought, "F****** hell, that's a long way from Norfolk to come to meet us". I didn't realise there was a Yarmouth on the Isle of Wight!

Next thing, without warning three Hawker Hunter planes flew right over us. Well if that was a welcome by the RAF, it wasn't one we enjoyed. Everyone dived to the floor. You had the ships' companies of three ships that had been bombed, and you send three planes to greet them without telling anyone.

I was greeted at Southampton docks QE2 terminal by my family and there were flags and banners with the names of many of us survivors on them. I saw one, 'Welcome Home Simon *HMS Antelope*' that I knew it was aimed for me.

12th June
My parents had previously been contacted by the local Colchester newspaper asking if they could come and interview me and gave a specific time which suited me as I was going shopping with my brother-in-law to buy some clothes as most of the clothes I owned went down with the *Antelope*. My Dad had just purchased a new speedboat and the reporter who turned up, late, first question was, "Have your parents bought you a new speedboat?"

I then went shopping with my brother-in-law and he was going to shops telling staff what had happened to me and how I have no clothes, asking if they could give me a discount. I was getting things like 2 for 1 jeans etc.

As we were walking down Colchester high street, a load of fighter planes flew over en route to some celebration in London, once again I dived on the floor.

Moving on to the day the war was declared over I got a phone call from a guy called David Woods. He said he was a reporter for a local paper and reminded me we had gone to school together and the conversation went along these lines.

"Hi Simon, it's David Woods. I work for the Colchester Gazette; can I have a chat? Are you glad the war is over?" and that was followed by "have you any plans to meet any mates when they return from the Falklands?" I made up a story that I've arranged to meet some mates of certain ships when they get back to Plymouth. The next day in the paper it was all changed around, quoting Portsmouth and other incorrect information I had given him!

After a few months, I was asked to attend a board of enquiry on the sinking of the *Antelope*. This was not a very pleasant experience; being grilled and questioned as to why I didn't know the starboard diesel generator had tripped (stopped) in the machinery space I was in charge of—apparently this caused loss of some of the ship's electrical power. I had to explain that I was lying down taking cover over the back of the other generator and was totally unaware it had tripped.

Later in 1982, I joined *HMS Herald*, a survey ship that was due to go to the Falklands the following year. Before we sailed me and a friend decided we would go on holiday to Majorca. We went a few months before we sailed and in a nightclub called Sinatra's I met some gorgeous young blonde girl. Her name was Jacqui. We met a few times before I sailed and wrote to each other all the time throughout my six months away.

On my return we got engaged and were married on 18th August 1984. We have been lucky to have two wonderful sons and a daughter. In memory of Mark, my mate who died on the *Antelope*, we named our second son after him, Jack Marcus.

I'll finish my story of the conflict by taking you back to when the landing craft from *HMS Fearless* came alongside to rescue us. Those guys were amazing but what happened to them later in the conflict completely shocked me and me shedding many, many tears.

I was at my parent's seaside flat when I heard the news that the landing craft had been hit by a bomb. The Argentine Air Force had just bombed *Sir Galahad* and what apparently happened was as they were flying back they dropped their bombs to ensure they could get back with the fuel they had left. The bomb exploded and killed 6 of the 8 crew members, including Dusty, the guy who gave me some overalls when we got to the *Fearless*.

HMS Antelope Explodes (Photo Martin Cleaver-Pool-Getty Images)

The Royal Marine Coxswain Colour Sergeant Brian Johnston was awarded a posthumous QGM for bravery. His citation reads:

"Colour Sergeant Johnston, the coxswain of LCU *F4*, was working in the vicinity of *HMS Antelope* when her unexploded bomb detonated, starting an immediate fire which caused her crew, already at emergency stations, to be ordered to abandon ship. Without hesitation, Colour Sergeant Johnston laid his craft alongside the *Antelope* and began to fight the fire and take off survivors. At approximately 2200hrs he was ordered to stay clear of the ship because of the severity of the fire and the presence of a second unexploded bomb. Colour Sergeant Johnston remained alongside until his load was complete. In all LCU *F4* rescued over 100 survivors from the *Antelope*.

Jim Prescott, the Army bomb disposal expert, was posthumously awarded The Conspicuous Gallantry Medal for his brave actions the only one awarded during the conflict. John Philips was awarded The Distinguished Service Cross for his bravery."

While on board the *QE2*, Simon filled out a drafting preference form as he was now without a ship. He specifically put that he did not want anything in Portsmouth as he hated it there, anywhere else was just fine. He was sent to Portsmouth to work at FMG.
    One day he was asked if he would like to go to Bermuda for two years. Sounded fantastic! Great, off you go and tell your wife. "Wife? I don't even have a girlfriend!" This was a draft for married personnel so that was swept out from under him just as quick.

Thankfully, another ship was given to him, he was to join the *Herald* and in this period of time he had met the woman who would later become his wife, so it wasn't all bad. What he also found was that *Herald* was about to be changing base port – to Devonport. But first he was heading south once again for a deployment to the Falklands.

By now it was over a year since he had survived *Antelope* and a memorial had been placed on the island for those lost during the conflict. They flew several of the lads out there to the memorial, but unfortunately they didn't pick them up for three hours and they stood there waiting in the freezing cold all that time.

Soon it was time to leave *Herald* and have a shore job at Northwood, although he was told at first to go back down to the South Atlantic. Thankfully the PO Writer sorted him out – he had had enough of that part of the world for the time being! He would now be in charge of servicing the fire equipment on the base.

Not long after he was given the job as the Killick stoker on the officer training ship *Sandpiper*, an ex-RAF target recovery vessel. Here the ship would be day-running to conduct serials and maybe travel over to places like Torquay or Jersey.

The one thing he remembers on here is that they had to take it in turns to cook the food. "The Skipper threw many meals back at me," he recalls. On one occasion he was expected to be providing a Sunday roast but what he made was Pizza with jacket potato – still with all the dirt on it from the field. Well, he did join up as an engineer, not a chef!

In 1987 he had got his rate for Petty Officer and was sent off to HMS Dryad overlooking Portsmouth, but by now he was starting a family and so did not want to carry on in the navy for much longer. Of course, once again, the Navy had other ideas – just a few months before he was due to leave, they told him he was to join a fishery protection vessel. Just before he was to join that he hurt his back in a sporting event and his draft was cancelled.

Simon left the Navy in 1989 and today has relinquished his hatred for Portsmouth, he now loves the place.

QE2 sails from Southampton

CPOMEA Martin "Barney" Barmby

I joined the Royal Navy as a Marine Engineering Mechanic 2nd class on the 16th of June 1986 at HMS Raleigh. I had followed my elder brother Peter into the RN as he had already been in nine years as a submariner, having served on O Boats and T boats as a MEM, LMEM and had become a POMEA(M).

Barney had previous experience in the Cadets and Territorial Army (TA)

An intense seven weeks of turning me from a civilian into a sailor followed, this task had been made a bit harder as I had four years army cadets and a year in the Territorial Army (TA) and as we all know army drill is a lot harder than navy drill! The RN must have seen something in me as I was made class leader throughout

Phase 1, 2 and 3 training, my time as a cadet Sergeant and a Lance Corporal in the TA may have helped!

After trade training to be a MEM (Marine Engineering Mechanic) at HMS Sultan I was sent to HMS Collingwood for the second to last MEM(L) (Marine Engineering Mechanic, Electrical) course to be held there before all ME training moved to HMS Sultan. On completion of Electrical training I was picked to be an SSMEM, a specially selected MEM for accelerated advancement to Leading Hand.

After completing my auxiliary machinery certificates on *HMS Illustrious* and my Fleet board for LMEM (Leading MEM), a year to the day after joining up I was passed for killick. A short time in Fleet Support at HMS Nelson followed after which in September 1987 I joined HMS Dolphin for basic submarine training as a volunteer, following my brother onto diesel electric submarines. I joined *HMS/m Otter* in January 1988 and after completing my Part 3 training to be a qualified submariner I stayed on *Otter* until September 1989 when I was sent back to HMS Sultan to complete LMEM(L) Qualifying course for six months, followed by Leading Rates Leadership course at HMS Royal Arthur for two weeks. Joining *HMS/m Opportune* in Plymouth just as she was leaving refit saw some interesting times, a full work up to war standards, making it to the Mediterranean

Sea for the first Gulf War to be turned round before the Suez Canal as the war had finished!

Barney (Centre) and co in aft mess, HMS Opportune.

Time spent spying on Colonel Gaddafi due to the trade embargo in force at that time, covert operations with SAS embarked and supporting NATO in the blockade of Yugoslavia/ Bosnia during that conflict.

Whilst on Staff College Sea Days with many high ranking officers on board we struck a Panamanian Cement freighter off the Isle of Wight in thick fog; they thought they had sunk us, but thankfully they had not, we sustained damage to our fore planes. The report in the Sun newspaper stated that, "Sailors heard a loud bang, followed by swearing!"

Options for change saw the RN get rid of all diesel submarines, after which I volunteered for Vanguard class submarines based in Faslane. A short stint on *MV Endeavour*, a tug in Faslane as its MEO (Marine Engineering Officer) before being drafted to HMS Sultan followed. I completed the second to last Marine

Engineering Artificers Candidate Course at HMS Sultan, finishing as an A/POMEA(EL)SM (Acting Petty Officer Marine Engineering Artificer (Electrical) Submarines). Three months in Rutherford block saw my conversion to a Nuclear Submariner, joining *HMS/m Vigilant* in January of 1998. I stayed on *Vigilant* until December 2000, completing four deterrent patrols.

Barney became an instructor later in his career.

Eighteen months shore side split between HMS Sultan and SMQ(N) (Submarine Qualification North) as an instructor, saw me return to *HMS Vigilant* as a CPOMEA(EL)SM (Chief Petty Officer Marine Engineering Artificer (Electrical) Submarines) completing a further three deterrent patrols. One of my last duties on board *Vigilant*, saw me save the life of a WOMEA2 (Warrant Officer Marine Engineering Artificer 2nd Class) who went against my advice and subsequently shorted out a spanner across live 440v terminal and suffered horrific burns. For my swift lifesaving actions I was awarded a Commander in Chief Fleets Commendation. I returned to SMQ(N) as an instructor in January 2005 and stayed there, finishing as lead instructor in August 2008 whence I de-mobbed.

During that time I acted as a sea rider taking a group of trainee submariners to the USA on *HMS/m Vanguard* after they had only done five weeks of a ten week course and all managed to qualify as submariners, a very proud time indeed.

November 2007 saw me awarded the Meritorious Service Medal for all the work I had undertaken with cadets outside my duties in the RN at Gosport, Helensburgh and Bridlington and my allegiance to the RNA (Royal Naval Assoc.) and RBL (Royal British Legion) whilst serving. On return to Bridlington I was heavily involved with the Royal Naval Section of the Combined Cadet Force at Bridlington School, which I commanded for three years as Lt(CCF)RNR (Lieutenant Combined Cadets Force, Royal Naval Reserves).

Barney is awarded the Meritorious Service Medal in 2007. Pictured with his parents and wife.

Following the closure of that unit last September Lt(SCC) (Lieutenant Sea Cadets Corps) Mikki Jackson and I have formed a Sea Cadet Unit in Bridlington that is heavily supported by the RNA of Bridlington. Within the RNA I have served as Chairman for five years and now hold the role of Standard Bearer. Having been a member of Bridlington RNA since 1989, I can honestly say the

overriding factor that makes it such a wonderful thing to be part of is the shipmates I have met, to a man and woman in these PC days I can honestly say I would have been honoured to serve with every one of them, having experienced the antics we get up to in the RNA, I am not sure, however, if I would have made it to Chief if I had known you lot in the mob! Once navy always navy.
RNA, its more than just a drinking club!

Barney (far left) at Bridlington cenotaph in one of many remembrance ceremonies for the Royal Naval Association and Royal British Legion.

I asked Barney about the incident that led to him being awarded a commendation and in turn led to him realising that his time in the Royal Navy was now up.

As the 23rd of November approaches my mind creeps back to ten years ago. I was the High Power Electrical Artificer on a Vanguard class submarine, a role I had held for over three years in total. I was asked by a WO2 (Warrant Officer 2nd Class) to lay forward and swap over the emergency AC diesel generator links from starboard to port whilst shutdown alongside in Faslane, a task I had never done but thought it can't be that hard. On getting to the switchboard in the AMS2 (Auxiliary Machinery Space 2) I worked out which links were live and which were dead.

  I realised removing the links from the dead side would not be a problem however was not so sure about replacing those links in the live side was an easy task. I rang the WO2 in the manoeuvring room to explain my situation and that I was going to dig out the relevant documentation and drawings relating to this job as I was not entirely confident in doing it live, I said it was doable but I was sure there must be an easier way.

  After putting the phone down I went to the Marine Engineering Technical Office, about ten metres from where I was working and found that there was no official operating instructions for doing the job I had been asked to do and the reason for that was common sense; there was no reason to do it with the connections live.

  As I returned to the switchboard the WO2 was already there swapping the links over. Three times I said if you drop one of those links or the spanner there will be a horrible bang, the lights will go out, you will be horribly burned. He ignored my advice and that of another WO2 who looked over his shoulder after I had explained he was operating when he should have been supervising and the second WO2 who said, "Barney has a point and you are a braver man than I gungardin!"

About thirty seconds later he shorted out a spanner between two 440v phases. He was horribly burned, suffered MRSA and did not hold his daughter until she was three months old (premature birth due to news of his injury). I administered some basic first aid to the WO2. A week after his injury I did try to visit him but got lost on the way to the hospital in Glasgow.

The next time I saw him it was just me and him walking towards each other on the main drag in Faslane and as I approached him he turned his head and ignored me. The next chance encounter would have been when I took naval cadets up to Faslane after I had left the RN and we were due to visit FASMAT (Faslane Manoeuvring Simulation Training), but he cancelled that visit as he was an instructor in FASMAT.

The first aid I carried out that day was down to training and not because of who he was; it was because I could. I expected no thanks but to be ignored still grips me. It was not an IED in Iraq or Afghanistan, a chest wound in Northern Ireland, but it was a moment in my service when I stood up to the mark and can hold my head up high and say I did my job and I did it well.

It crosses my mind every time I go into the switchboards at work about how stupid he was and how avoidable it was. It was however a deciding factor into my leaving the RN when those in positions of authority totally disregard your ideas without a thought. Sometimes the people that do the job day in day out may just be more up to date and experienced than you and it won't hurt to at least listen.

When asked "Why did you join the navy?"... Barney replied

My elder brother appearing at home three or four times a year with exotic gifts from across the globe! I thought, I'll have some of that!

Do you regret leaving?

Sometimes yes, the work ethic and teamwork in civvy street is s***, I don't miss the sea time though.

Barney was awarded a commendation for his life saving actions after the incident on board HMS Vigilant.

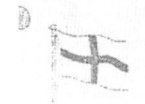

By Admiral Sir Jonathon Band, Knight Commander of the Order of the Bath. Admiral in Her Majesty's Fleet and Commander in Chief of Her Majesty's Ships and Vessels employed and to be employed in the Fleet.

COMMANDER-IN-CHIEF FLEET'S COMMENDATION

Chief Petty Officer Marine Engineering Artificer Barmby

On 23 November 2004, during HMS VIGILANT's planned maintenance period at HM Naval Base Clyde, part of the work package included the realignment of interconnecting links within a switchboard on the Main AC Electrical Distribution System. During this process, the maintainer accidentally created a short circuit across two phases of the supply and received a major electric shock. The short circuit passed through the maintainer's right arm, torso and right leg, resulting in major burns and open wounds as well as severe flash burns to his face and head. Fortunate to be alive, the maintainer was barely conscious and in deep shock.

Present in the vicinity at the time of the incident, Chief Petty Officer Barmby immediately raised the alarm as the switchboard filled with smoke and engulfed the maintainer. In full knowledge of the associated hazards and without regard for his personal safety, he entered the smoke filled switchboard and pulled the maintainer to safety. Aware of the potential effects of electrical burns, he immediately administered first aid action, removing the maintainer's smoldering clothing and taking him to the nearest source of water. He continued to douse the burns in cold water until Medical Staff arrived and, despite having sustained burn injuries himself, he continued to assist with the medical care until an ambulance arrived.

Barmby demonstrated his ability to remain calm and take decisive life-saving action under stressful conditions throughout this incident. His initial actions, conducted without hesitation or fear for himself, undoubtedly enhanced the maintainer's chances of surviving the incident. His subsequent first aid actions were conducted with an exceptionally clear head and presence of mind, greatly reducing the impact of the maintainer's burns. These actions, highly praised by the staff at Glasgow Royal Infirmary Burns Unit, are most fittingly recognised by the award of my Commendation.

Admiral Sir Jonathon Band KCB

Robert Lawes
ex CPOET(WE) 1993 to 2015

One of the overriding memories that has stayed with me since the day I saw it, around 20 years ago, took place one Wednesday morning at HMS Collingwood. It has stayed with me, not only because it's funny but it highlights triumph in adversity, military humour and quick thinking.

I joined the RN in August 1993 as an Operator Mechanic Communications 2nd Class. We were the very first entrants into the brand new "Warfare Branch". To say the decision to merge the weapons engineering department with the operations branch, to create this new group, had been an unpopular one would be a massive understatement.

By the year 2000 I'd managed to be selected for Artificer training and had joined Collingwood in the May as AC996 entry. Anyone who has spent any length of time at Collingwood will have less than fond memories of Wednesday mornings. Every Wednesday at 07:00 all the career courses troop out to the parade ground and stand around for half an hour waiting to fall in and then march out on to the square for ceremonial division practice. Every week the march past the inspecting officer normally ended in farce for several classes who would then be given the dreaded "red card" and sent around again and invited back for re-training at lunch times.

On this one, grey, south coast morning, we'd all marched out in our classes and were stood at ease waiting for the divisional officers to pitch up.

Marching smartly between the divisions, bawling out instructions and rebukes was a Sergeant Royal Marines. The man was every inch his profession. Tall, sporting a fine moustache, every crease razor sharp, boots gleaming, and pace stick polished and clamped under his arm.

As he marched between the ranks of the waiting divisions, I noticed his head snap around to look at a member of one of the squads off to my left. In a loud voice he boomed out, "You lad, I can see you moving, stand still, I've got eyes in the back of my head."

Just as he'd finished saying that he walked smack into the rear man of the division in front of us sending him sprawling.

The Sergeant, paused, checked his uniform, straightened up, clamped his pace stick back under his arm and, in a loud clear voice added… "Shame I haven't got them in the front though," and marched off to continue his rounds.

The sound of laughter rang out from all who saw and heard what had happened.

"Silence…" came the cry and you could have heard a pin drop.

It's moments like that which highlight the humour and spirit of servicemen and women.

Richard Jones

I was only a lad of 17 when I thought seriously about joining the Royal Navy. Born in Leeds but moving to Bridlington at 13, I left school with grades that were... OK. They weren't amazing but to be honest I didn't care; I had a job near the harbour at JC's Restaurant and I was sorted. But a year after leaving school life was so boring, I had no time to do what I wanted and I was working six days a week. I had always had an interest in ships ever since watching 'Raise the Titanic' as a child; since then I had been obsessed with the sea.

So one day I was discussing the prospect of going to sea on cruise liners or ferries and the chef turned around to me and said, "Why don't you join the Royal Navy... oh no, maybe not... I don't think you would hack it."

I don't know if she said it on purpose to get me motivated or not (I suspect it was just a throwaway comment) but it sparked off a feeling of "course I could hack it" and off I went to the Job Centre to find out how the hell I joined the Royal Navy.

It was not long before I was given the date for an interview and so I made sure that was my day off and headed down to the careers office in Hull.

A fifty minute train ride later and I was at the office looking at posters of what looked like someone dressed up in firefighting gear about to battle a raging inferno. Well that didn't look fun. Before long I was called in and sat down at a desk with about 20-30 others; we had a basic Maths and English test to do, which I completed and then we all sat in silence.

It wasn't long before someone came in and said, "You, you and you... follow me please."

My first thought was that they had made it through and we all hadn't, but then he came back a few minutes later and said, "Right, the rest of you have passed."

I breathed a sigh of relief and was once again called into an office, this time for a one-to-one chat. A Chief Petty Officer John McDougal sat me down and started by asking me what the ship was in the photograph on the wall. I guessed frigate; I guessed wrong. OK so my ocean liner knowledge was better than my warship.

He then asked me what I considered smart clothing – at this point I realised I was in a bright red V-neck jumper, T-shirt and trousers. "Is this acceptable for a job interview?" he said. I didn't dare tell him that I didn't possess a suit and on my wages I never would!

"Do you go out clubbing?"
"No."
"Do you go swimming?"
"No."
"Do you go to the gym?"
"No."
"Do you go to the cinema?"
"Oh yes!"
"What have you seen?"
"I have seen Titanic four times!" I said proudly.
"Anything else?"
"Erm... No."

It was obvious that I was living a sheltered life and one that gave me absolutely no social life whatsoever, but at this point I thought this interview was going so badly he was going to kick me out of the door.

"Right, I'm going to take this into my office, flower it up a bit and have a good cry," he said.

Incredibly, he then sent me to have a medical examination and told me my Maths and English test had come back really good. After having a stint with the doctor and a McDonalds with two of the guys who had also made it through, I went back to Brid and went back to work the next day. I didn't dare tell anybody what I was doing, I was afraid they would laugh at me and if they told me that I hadn't made it I would have never lived it down.

But two days before my 18th birthday (October 1998) came the news that I was to be laid off and so for the first time I had to head to the Job Centre to sign on the dole, but by now I didn't care. I had received a letter telling me that I was to join the Royal Navy as an Operator Mechanic 2nd Class on 30th November 1998. In less than two months I was on a train to Plymouth wondering what the hell I had done and if I would make it through the training.

So, on 29th November I arrived at Plymouth station to be met by a guy advertising himself as Navy so from that moment on I knew I'd be OK, just follow and do as he says. Simple!

A bus down to the Torpoint ferry, off the bus, onto the clanky vessel that is pulled along on chains, back on another bus on the opposite side and a short drive to the gates of HMS Raleigh.

For the next twelve days we were given our kit and taught all the traditions, sayings and marks of respect that we would need and made to run everywhere. The physical training was intense and I won't lie I hated it, but the camaraderie was amazing. For once I had a whole group of new friends from all different backgrounds who regarded me as one of them. Unfortunately after having a flu shot I got the flu really bad (coincidence?) and by the time we went on Christmas leave on 12th December I was in a bad state, spending the next few days in bed being unable to speak. Thankfully, I recovered OK and enjoyed my time off, then back to Raleigh to complete the next six weeks.

More marching practice, assault courses, obstacle course, Dartmoor, spraining my ankle where I had to hobble behind the class for two weeks, then finally on 12th February 1999 our class, Cunningham 49, passed out as the Guard and we could finally say that we had completed basic training.

Richard "Jonah" Jones at HMS Raleigh (back row, far left)

The night before we passed out we were expecting a visit from "Captain Counterpane" which was basically one of the other classes wearing nothing but boxer shorts and gas masks and swinging their boots at anybody that moved, led by a guy wearing his bed counterpane as his cape. Laid there that night we heard them all coming down the stairs and prepared for them to burst through the door and start attacking. But suddenly everything went silent and a shout from the duty PO doing rounds, "What the hell are you lot doing?" Needless to say, we all laughed ourselves to sleep.

Another funny occasion happened as the lights went out one night and two of the lads thought it would be a good idea to have a pillow fight in the dark. They were proper battering each other with them and making noises like a knackered tennis player, again the duty PO suddenly made an appearance at the door and screamed at them both. Muffled laughter could be heard from everybody not moving a muscle in their beds!

I met some great people while I was there, some I am still friends with today, especially since Facebook has reconnected me with many of them. The problem back in the 90's was that when you deployed you would never find out if your oppo had changed his mobile phone number and so one by one you would lose touch.

Sadly our class was now going to split up; engineers went off to their next course, we were seamen so we had to do another four weeks of seamanship training at Raleigh before we too were once again split up and I was sent to HMS Collingwood in Fareham to learn communications.

The course was alright, nothing too exciting. A week of leadership training in Tal-y-Bont which wasn't my cup of tea, but it was an experience. After the course it was Basic Sea Survival Course – or BSSC – where we learned damage control and firefighting techniques. I remember one of the fire instructors being a right horrible git to the students, speaking to them like crap. I was glad to be out of there. I later found out that a guy working there at the time had murdered two people and is suspected of killing more. I noticed a missing poster at Raleigh for a young sailor who had gone missing in Portsmouth; it was only when Petty Officer Alan Grimson was arrested did they find both him and a second body (a pub barman). Scary when you think you don't know really who you are serving with!

So as my training was finally coming to an end, the PO instructor, Al Gower, told me that I had got the *Sutherland* as my first ship. I had put down for an aircraft carrier or Type 42 destroyer, anything but a Type 23 frigate. *Sutherland* was a Type 23. Anyway, I went over to find out the ships program and was disappointed to see she was going to Ipswich and then doing BOST – Basic Operational Sea Training. Several weeks of hell where the Flag Officer Sea Training (FOST) staff scream at you while holding clip boards. PO Gower saw me later and asked how I felt about it. "Ah, it's OK I guess," I said trying to be as enthusiastic as I could.

A day later he saw me again and told me that my draft had changed. "You're on the *Northumberland*, find out where that's going," he said.

I could not believe it! She was already out in the Caribbean doing drug patrols and due back at Christmas. Talk about a great first draft!

The Navy picked me up in a car from Collingwood early one September morning and drove me to, I think it was, Gatwick. There I was given tickets to a British Airways Business Class seat to Barbados which was amazing! I then took a flight island hopping from Barbados to St Kitts where I was to meet the ship. But a PO who was going on draft himself from the ship met me at the airport to tell me that she had already sailed to Puerto Rico to conduct a repair on the RADAR system. I had to stay in a hotel overnight before taking another flight the next day where I was then met by a Chief Switalski who drove me to the US Navy base at Roosevelt Roads. I was shocked at just how big it was... we seemed to be driving ages before we reached the ship, I was convinced we were not on a base anymore!

Jones first ship - HMS Northumberland

When I finally reached the *Northumberland*, it was an incredible experience, we sailed the day after and over the next few months I would learn everything about my job, the ship and the people on board.

The first thing you learn is that you are prone to "bites" when you are new. A bite is when someone tricks you into either believing something stupid or doing something for everyone to laugh at. My personal favourite was the time the Yeoman (PO Steve Kelly – a great guy!) gave me an axe to give to the Buffer, but first I had to hand him an envelope. Off I went down 2-deck, knocked on the PO's mess door, handed him the envelope and he stood there reading it. "Do you know what this says?" he asked me. Obviously I didn't, but I soon found out.

*Give me a make n mend or I'll chop your f****ng head off.*

The Buffer knelt down and put his neck to the floor and said, "No you f***ing can't!" I laughed for ages about this and the Yeoman found it hilarious.

Years later I did the same to the new guy on one of the mine hunters, unfortunately the Buffer was chatting to the Captain at the time! Thankfully, he saw the funny side of it.

So the Caribbean patrols were good, we visited some great places; the first one for me was Trinidad, going alongside Port-of-Spain and seeing the half sunken shipwrecks in the harbour. I paid a guy to take me out in a little wooden boat so that I could take photos of them, it was well worth it and something that nobody else had done on board.

Martinique was probably the most boring of the islands, everything shut on a Sunday as it was owned by the French. Anguilla had me crawling over cliffs to get to two more shipwrecks, some good adventures there and more great photos. I had to avoid so many insects that were constantly buzzing around in the extreme heat. I did take a couple of nutty bars with me but they had already melted.

The Can Man (Canteen Manager) had brought in loads of Mounds bars; I'm not going to lie they were disgusting. Imagine a Bounty, but a really, really cheaply made version. People were hoping they would run out so that he would get some proper chocolate in but they seemed to last forever. I heard they were used in raffle prizes and some just bought then to chuck overboard to get rid of them!

One day we stopped a cargo ship like we had done countless times in the last month, called the *Adriatik*. The ship was suspicious so we had to board her and make sure she wasn't smuggling. Volunteers were required to go over and help shift these huge bags of sugar in the cargo hold in order to expose the fuel tanks, apparently a trick they use is to fill the tanks up with drugs then smear diesel over the hatch so that nothing is detected.

It was so hot in there as each bag was a 2-man lift, humping them one by one into a pile until all the covers were ready to open. At this point we turned the ship over to the US Coastguard who informed us the next day that we had caught a ship that was smuggling cocaine, £137 million of it! This was a great victory for us and one that got us in the papers and Navy News. At last I felt like I was doing something useful with my life.

November was also hurricane season, and one ship in particular was finding the weather too much. The *Pride La Dominique* was taking on water and had suffered engine failure, so we were tasked to take the ship in tow and bring her to a safe spot that was sheltered. We were all split up into teams and each team would do their assigned part of the towing before moving away and allowing the next team to proceed. It worked like clockwork and the ship was slowly but surely making her way to Anguilla where we had only been a few months before.

When I woke up the following morning there were a small bunch of Caribbean looking guys in the Junior Rates Dining Hall, I found out soon enough that they had come from the *Pride La Dominique* as they had to be rescued when the ship was safely in the bay but had then drifted onto the rocks. When I went up top the storm had long passed, but on the cliffs were the two wrecks that I had explored a few weeks ago, with one addition! I believe the ship was taken off the cliffs in the end and is still in service today. After the hurricanes had passed, our lads went over in a helicopter to assist locals with the damage to their homes. I didn't participate in that but I heard it was not nice.

So with a big drug bust and some hurricane rescue operations under our belt we headed back to Devonport, a slow sailing across the Atlantic where the electronic chart table was switched off so that the officers could navigate the old fashioned way. I hoped they were better than my steering; I got the ship half a mile off course in a flat calm in less than an hour!

December 1999, we came alongside to the cheers of the families and the promise of Christmas leave. It was a great trip but for now we were going to be alongside for quite a while as we had maintenance to do on the ship in the January and February of the new Millennium.

By around September time of 2000 we were deployed again, this time to the Mediterranean where we were participating in various exercises. An exercise the previous May almost ended in collision with a French frigate (good bridge teams on both ships prevented a disaster) and had some more great runs ashore.

Toulon in France where one of the lads was sprayed in the face with something and so the rest of the lads chased the guy who did it. Barcelona (Spain) where me and a couple of the girls went up the Sagrada Familiar, Gaudi's unfinished church. Limassol in Cyprus where I went with my friend Cheryl to explore the town of Paphos. It was here we did paragliding, took a trip on a glass bottomed boat over a shipwreck and hired a speedboat out to see a cargo ship that had run aground.

Exercises are dull at the best of times but thankfully the runs ashore and the fun times break up the monotony and once again we had a great welcome home in the December. But this was the end of my draft for my taskbook was complete and I was to be promoted to OM1

(Operator Mechanic First Class) which meant I would be sent to Collingwood for a few months to do a course and then earn the star on my arm.

OM(C)1 course 2001 (Richard is back row, third from the left)

       The first few months of 2001 was taken up by flashing light training, electronics and Weapons Engineering basics and more comms principles. Nothing too drastic but once again made more new friends and before we knew it we had our drafts – I was back on a Type 23 frigate, this time *HMS Montrose* which was Devonport based. But as I had already been on a Guzz based 23 I wanted something Portsmouth way due to it taking less time to head up home to Yorkshire and it was close to the town and museums that I loved so much.

       Several people had been given the old Landing Platform Dock *HMS Fearless*, a steam powered crate that had caught fire pretty bad the year before and was still being repaired. I offered to swap draft and it was accepted, so in the May of 2001 I packed my bags and joined the "Cheerless" which was alongside in Portsmouth. I was taken down into 3C1 mess, two decks below the fo'c'sle hatch, which was a thin mess square with seating all around and a small wooden door leading to nine beds in rows of three.

It soon became apparent that I had made a huge mistake in swapping. The people on *Fearless* were not welcoming when it came to an OM(C)1 on board, for they were all "source branch" radio operators (RO's), some being in the navy over twenty years as an AB (Able Seaman). It became apparent that they were all put on the Fearless in order to operate all the old equipment (the ship had been launched in 1963) but they seemed very bitter about not only their life choices but being on the ship with these new guys.

Thankfully my new task book was full of WE jobs so I was sent over to work with the engineers for a while and after that I was Senior Rates Messman for a few months, so that kept me away from most of them. The problem with a ship like this was the tribal messing – if you didn't get along with the people you worked with it was tough, they would also be living in the same mess as you. All comms guys were in one of two messdecks, so you didn't mix with anybody else on board unless your paths crossed in the nature of your work.

Following BOST (Basic Operational Sea Training), we deployed for Exercise Saif Sareer II (Shining Sword II) which was off Oman and the journey took us through the Med and headed to Turkey. But things were about to change for us in a way we couldn't possibly imagine.

It was 11th September 2001 and RO Dusty Miller came into the mess and told us that hijacked planes had crashed into the World Trade Center in New York and another into the Pentagon, both towers had collapsed. It seemed so far-fetched that I left the mess and headed up to the MCO (Main Communications Office). If anything like this had happened they would know about it. I walked in and asked how they were, RO Stu Ellison looked at me and said, "Haven't you heard?"

"Oh, is it true?" I asked, shocked. Turns out it was.

We tried to get the crappy dial-up satellite internet up and working to check the BBC News website and a picture loaded up of the plane hitting the tower and every one of us was like, "wooooaaaahhh!"

After that we went alongside Marmaris in Turkey as planned where I learned to dive for the first time and got my PADI Open Water qualification. After several days here we left for the exercise via the Suez Canal and were then told that we would not be home for Christmas as we would be assisting with the marines deploying to Afghanistan. As the first bombing raids were hitting the Taliban compounds, we all wondered what was going to be in store for us. But travelling south down the Red Sea we had a failure of our air conditioning, so the heat built up inside the ship to the point where we were constantly sweating no matter what we did. This even made the papers back home as I later found out.

The exercise went ahead, followed by real-life operations; to be honest it was boring as hell. We'd flood the back of the ship, the huge door would open, the landing craft floated out and that was our job done until it was time for the craft to come back.

Other than a leg-stretch on a deserted Omani beach, we spent 52 days at sea before we got into Diego Garcia in the middle of the Indian Ocean. We crossed the line and had the usual ceremony of being "shaved" and force fed dog biscuits and then being dunked backwards into a pool of water. I had been baptised by King Neptune, as had half the ships company.

When my time as Mess Man came to an end it was back into the MCO (Main Communications Office) to work with the RO's (Radio Operators) again. Thankfully a female killick had joined who was much more approachable and was more than happy to take me through the training and general things that I didn't know, bearing in mind the kit was 1960s and I had only been taught on modern day kit.

Christmas in Dubai, 2001

As we spent Christmas and New Year into 2002 alongside Dubai, we were eventually told that we will return in March and that will be the last time *Fearless* will be at sea. I was loaned to the Type 23 frigate *HMS Kent* for nine days before flying back to *Fearless* and once again we made our way out of the Gulf, up the Red Sea and into Barcelona.

HMS Fearless in Barcelona, it's last ever port visit (March 2002) before decommissioning

On 17th March 2002 we came into Portsmouth for the final time, a fly past of helicopters and hundreds cheering on the jetty. There were TV cameras, Falklands veterans and the families of the people on board, it was fantastic. Then it was all over. We had done seven months away and now we were on leave for several weeks before coming back and doing literally nothing.

I must have spent days just sat watching TV in the mess, now and again we'd get an odd job then it was back to the telly. The ship was getting decommissioned so there was no point repairing anything unless it was needed. Bit by bit, kit was getting taken off and carried away in lorries to be used elsewhere in the fleet. Before long I had been given a draft to the Type 23 *HMS Grafton*, so it was now time to prepare to leave the ship.

In June I walked off the ship and weeks later stepped on the *Grafton*, ready to deploy once again to the Caribbean, my second deployment in just a few months.

The West Indies trip was one of my better trips in the Navy; we did three drug busts in just four months - £7.5 million of cannabis from the speedboat *Roma J*, £500,000 of cannabis from the wooden "go-fast" *OHB* and £100 million of cocaine from the fishing vessel *Genesis I*.

That big one was interesting because that gave us a headline hitting haul but the boat rolled over in the night and the following morning

Genesis I alongside HMS Grafton October 2002 where £100 million of cocaine was discovered.

we were using her as target practice in order to sink it, otherwise it would be a navigation hazard. Unfortunately, these type of boats are made from polystyrene, apparently within the hull, so she just floated there full of bullet holes until we had to just report it on as a nav hazard.

One day my mate was up on the bridge when he spotted a guy in a speedboat waving his oar in the air.

When the ship turned around and picked him up he was stick thin and very ill; he had lost power to his boat and had been at sea for weeks! As we airlifted him to hospital we tested his boat and it proved that he had once had cocaine on board. We heard a rumour that he ran from the hospital later and was wanted for murder. No idea if there was any truth in these though, matelot dits sometimes get out of hand!

During my three years on the *Grafton* I was lent out to the UK Maritime Component Commander at Bahrain to operate the comms system, that was Christmas away from home but it was an enjoyable three months.

We deployed back to the Gulf twice, where I visited so many other places including a lot that I had done before – Gibraltar, Bahrain, Dubai, Salalah, Malta – and even managed to upgrade my diving qualifications to Rescue Diver.

But unfortunately the people were now starting to get on my nerves. I was sick to death of being treated like crap by some of the ship's company, especially my bosses, and the constant threats of being disciplined when you hadn't done anything wrong (there was a threat on Daily Orders every day).

I handed in my twelve months' notice and did a resettlement course out in Egypt to become a qualified Dive Master. It was no problem finding a job on the outside and I bought my own flat ready for me to be a civilian.

The last few days of my naval career I spent in my mate's cabin; it was the 200th anniversary of Trafalgar in 2005 and at the end of June they had a huge fireworks display in the Solent. I never did understand why they did it in June (the battle was fought in October), but it was good to see and a great ending. Handing over my ID card, I was given a veteran's badge and a certificate of discharge and, after six years and seven months service, I walked out of the gates of HMS Nelson and off I went on the train back to Yorkshire.

I was happy to be free of the Navy and I did leave hating it, but after a year of being in civvy street I realised that life in a small town on the East Yorkshire coast was boring as hell. I never fell out of love with all the things to do with the Royal Navy, I just hated working for them.

Richard Jones on Grafton flashing light with another ship.

But as time went on, the friends that I had when I used to come home on leave didn't want to know me anymore (my nice big fat wage had been drastically reduced and so I wasn't buying rounds of drinks every Saturday night any more). I was trying to write my first book and funding for research was scarce. I seemed to be working ten times harder for a wage that left me with barely anything to live on after bills.

After several incidents involving friends and family turning their backs on me I made a drastic and life changing decision – I would re-join the Royal Navy. Only this time I would have a completely different attitude.

In September 2007 I once again walked through the gates of HMS Raleigh for the welcome back and a few days administration and paperwork. By the November I was back on a ship ready to deploy the following January.

Joining HMS Richmond, Brest, 2014

So, what had changed? Well for one I did not stand for bullying any more, never again would I be treated like crap by some jumped up killick or PO with a power trip. I am not afraid of sticking up for myself when it comes to what is right, and that goes for the lads too – I have their back.

I have now embraced the perks that come with being a matelot – the free courses, adventurous training, opportunities to do ceremonial, using the gym, taking photos of the places I visit, the list is endless.

Today I am approaching twenty years served and a lot has changed – my branch (I am now a Weapons Engineer), my rank (I finally got to Leading Hand… eventually), the deployments (thirteen of them), the ships (served on thirteen of them) and the people. I not only managed to complete my book that I was writing but I have now published eleven more!

Over the years I have seen so many good people leave the Navy, but for now I am staying put. I still have many more adventures on my list before I become a civvy again, no doubt that list will grow over time. By then I may write my memoirs fully.

Richard Jones at sea in 2020 on board HMS Westminster

Sam Shannon

Tell me why you joined the navy.

I joined the Navy 29th April 2012 because I wanted to see the world. Whilst on Public Services course at college the Navy came and gave us a presentation on why to join so I thought, yeah I'll do it that. So, I'll get to see the world and think about what I want to do whilst I'm in.

You became a Weapons Engineer. Where did that lead you?

After Phase Two training I went into holdover in Guzz where I worked for SFP, a submariner Towed Array team. We went on two jollys to Fujairah and Gibraltar where we would meet the Submarine on the way into port, remove its towed array and reel it up. We would then reconnect it when it left.

Tell me about your first ship. Did you go anywhere nice?

I spent three years on *HMS Lancaster* and carried out two deployments. My first was to the Caribbean APT(N) (Atlantic Patrol Tasking North), carrying out Counter-Drug smuggling operations and Disaster Relief. My second was APT(S) (Atlantic Patrol Tasking South), where we went down to the Falkland Islands. Note to self... do not go there during Winter, everything is cancelled. When we got back we stripped *Lancaster* down to its knees ready to scrap it before the ships company left it alongside *HMS Dauntless*.

HMS Lancaster

You then picked up your rate, where did you end up after Killicks Course?

I then joined *HMS Westminster* where I enjoyed many day working films whilst everyone slept and worked hard. You would often find me as confused as Jonah (the author) looking at the same bit of Comms, normally Infra Red. It was on here that I decided to leave the Navy to live a normal life where I could go home every evening and make memories with my family.

What memories of your time in the Navy stand out the most?

During my leave period I went on holiday to Thailand. As we were going down a busy main road in Bangkok, a scooter caught our eye as it had the Dad driving, the Mum behind feeding a new born baby and to top it off there was a three year old sat on the back facing the opposite way casually eating a yoghurt. Mind blown.

One time on the *Lancaster* the stokers were removing the poo pipe from above the 39 man mess hatch and as they removed it one of the MEs lowered their end slightly and looked up, as he looked up he opened his mouth without realising and poo came out of the pipe and fell right into his mouth, he was gaging like mad whilst everyone else was in stitches.

On the same ship, we were anchored off the Cayman Islands using a ferry to get to and from the ship/shore. The last ferry was at 2am and that would be it until

Sam Shannon on HMS Lancaster in 2015

8am. Two of the lads missed the last ferry so decided to take a taxi to the closest point to the ship. They then tried to swim back to ship with their wallet and phone in their mouths. They were being pulled out by the current and would have drowned if Whiskey (one of the comms guys) wasn't having a fag at the time. He heard them shouting and he then called "man overboard." They were rescued and brought to the steps where you go down to get on the ferry. The Captain was waiting at the top of the steps and was not in a happy mood.

One of the same guys who tried to swim back to ship in the Cayman Islands messed up again in Colombia. But this time it was for a different reason as we were alongside. He was adrift, it was around 8am when he rocked up near the ship with another lad. They had found leaf blowers on their way back and had decided they were the Ghostbusters, so were running and rolling around pretending to suck up ghosts whilst singing the song. As this was happening the Captain was watching them from the Bridge with some binoculars. After a few minutes of watching them and laughing he told some of the crew to get them back onboard.

You must have served with some real characters during your time.

Yes! During BOST, a WE (Weapons Engineer) was carrying out blanket searches and a FOSTY said, "There's a fire in there, what are you going to do?" The WE shut the door and carried on his blanket search. The FOSTY said, "What are you doing?" to which he replied "Carrying out my blanket search. That room's not on my sheet."

Sam left the Navy in 2020 and is now an engineer working for a big company in Portsmouth that works closely with the navy, but he gets to go home and spend time with his family every night. He has no regrets.

Epilogue

This book started out as a way to get people talking about their time in the Royal Navy while they were stuck at home during lockdown period. In just a few months over a dozen people had got in touch and many of them were happy for their stories to be published so that their life at sea could be forever laid down in print.

Some of the people interviewed had lots to say, others just wanted to tell me their best dit or ones that made them laugh at the time. For example, Peter Nicholas Derby Allen recalls a main broadcast pipe on board HMS Bulwark in 1970 - "For all those that need to do so may now do so over the starboard side." Ship turned out of wind cos we had no Heads working.

The Royal Navy is not all fun and games, sometimes it can be very hard work, sometimes it can be downright depressing. Being away from family can hit some people harder than others, especially for newlyweds or those who have recently become parents. But this is a job that is like no other. You sail away from the country you love, work with other navies, visit foreign lands and see things that people back on dry land could only ever dream about.

There are skills you learn that never leave you, people you meet that become friends for life and memories that never fade away.

I am lucky that the people who agreed to contribute to this book range in years from the 1950s right up to the present day. This is a cross section of people, years, ships, jobs and world events. We can only wonder now what it was like during the First World War, all the veterans have passed on. But we still have the chance to gather all the stories from the Second World War, there is time to speak to veterans of the Falklands conflict and learn from those who fought in Iraq and Afghanistan.

It will only be a matter of time before war is on the horizon once again, there is never peace for too long, but no matter who is right and who is wrong the people of the navies of the world are there on the front line. In 1982 the British and Argentine people were enemies, but in 2018 they worked closely together in the search for the lost Argentinean submarine *San Juan* which had vanished in the South Atlantic. Tragically she was found a year later with the loss of all 44 of her crew, but this showed that common arguments can be put to one side in order to achieve a mission.

The Royal Navy may not always be in the headlines, but behind closed doors they are doing a lot more than people think. Drug busting in the Caribbean, exercising with NATO units in mid-Atlantic, fishery protection in UK waters, mine hunting in the English Channel (there are still things out there from the wars) and survey operations in the Gulf.

While the navy has changed a lot since the Second World War, the fundamental aspects remain the same. The ships are still away at sea and the daily maintenance of these vessels takes place along with all other duties. One of the most memorable things a sailor can do is march on parade on Armed Forces Day and Remembrance Day when the public show their appreciation openly and the flags fly free with patriotic pride.

A lot of talk has been had regarding the size of the Royal Navy and compared to the Cold War there has been a huge reduction in both seagoing units, shore bases and personnel. But today we have two of the most modern aircraft carriers in the world, a new building program of nuclear submarines, offshore patrol vessels and Type 26, Type 31 and now recently announced Type 32 frigates.

Ships and their sailors have continued to operate throughout the COVID-19 pandemic, sometimes at great sacrifice and risk to themselves in such confined conditions and spending unexpected months at a time away from loved ones. Unlike a planned deployment, COVID-19 has given no 'deployment end date' or homecoming to count down to seeing their families again. You may not always read about what they are involved in, and when you do it is often misrepresented, but rest assured they are out there.

In 10-20 years' time there will be new stories to gather, new navy memories and hopefully more positive news stories to look back on.

But for now we can look back on these stories of the matelots of years gone by and we can all enjoy their Royal Navy experiences together.

In the meantime, if you are ever in the area of a naval base and you see one of Her Majesty's finest warships leaving port, make sure you stop and give them a wave.

The future of the Royal Navy - The aircraft carriers HMS Queen Elizabeth and HMS Prince of Wales in Portsmouth in 2020

Printed in Great Britain
by Amazon